For This Marvelous Country

Counting on me to get them back home

By Carol Rose Offutt

For This Marvelous Country

Copyright © 2009 by Carol Rose Offutt

All rights reserved. No part of this book may be reproduced or transmitted in any form or by any means without written permission from the author.

The text in this book was typed with a comfortable font and line spacing to accommodate our elder veterans.

ISBN 13: 978-0-615-33605-3
ISBN 10: 0-615-33605-1

Dedication

To my family,
Thank you for sharing this loving journey.
My heart is full.

Table of Contents

Chapter One	1941	1
Chapter Two	Oath	5
Chapter Three	First Crew	12
Chapter Four	European Theater	17
Chapter Five	"Black Thursday"	24
Chapter Six	Life after Schweinfurt	34
Chapter Seven	Back in the States	50
Chapter Eight	Invitation	59
Chapter Nine	Lockbourne	70
Chapter Ten	Accidents	83
Chapter Eleven	New Crew	88
Chapter Twelve	1945	101
Chapter Thirteen	Europe	107
Chapter Fourteen	Army of Occupation	118
Chapter Fifteen	Dance	140

Acknowledgements

Chapter One

1941

After spending twenty-four months as an engineer in a Nicaraguan mining camp, Bill knew it was time for him to make a change.

He knew if he returned home to the States he would have to register for the draft and would probably be drafted immediately. Signs of war were everywhere.

There was a lot of construction going on in Panama at the time. A former mine superintendent asked Bill to come to Panama and work for him. If he worked in Panama, Bill would still have to register for the draft, but would be exempt because he would be doing government commissioned work.

Bill needed little convincing. He was moving to Panama, the country he had loved as a young boy.

It was time for my farewell party. Smitty, Carlos and I decided to have a cocktail party, Sunday afternoon, December 7, 1941.

When everything was ready for the party I turned on the radio for background music. Imagine my surprise when I heard that Costa Rica had declared war on Japan. I couldn't believe it!

I called Smitty and Carlos over to the radio. We started dialing other stations and then got one with the news that Japan had attacked the United States' fleet at Pearl Harbor.

As our guests arrived, they crowded around the radio with us. We discussed what the attack would mean to each of us and to the mining company. The party should have ended with the horrifying news reports, but no one could bear to leave their friends. We clung to each other not knowing our fate.

The next morning I changed my plans. Panama was no longer an option for me. I needed to go home to New Orleans.

I flew by TACA Airlines to Puerto Cabezas, on the East coast of Nicaragua. While in Puerto Cabezas, I visited our chief electrician who was taken from the mine by soldiers. He was a German fellow interned by the Nicaraguan government. They interned all Japanese and Germans to prevent sabotage, spying or aiding others that might be plotting against the government, the people or structures. They copied the United States, interning all Japanese and their descendants on the West coast without recourse to a legal system. The insecurity of the government was beginning to be felt by all the people. What if they were right?

From Puerto Cabezas, I caught passage on a Standard Fruit and Steamship Company ship. The vessel stopped at La Ceiba, Honduras, and from there, continued on to New Orleans.

I had the radio operator send a cable to my parents that I was on my way home. My dad, who worked for Standard Fruit and Steamship Company, later told me the operator was penalized for sending that message because a German submarine in the Gulf of Mexico could have honed in on the transmission and torpedoed the ship.

Torpedo the ship! I was so perplexed. The Gulf of Mexico was where, as a youngster, I earned my Sea Scout badges. Those waters could not handle wartime submarines, could they?

Chapter Two

Oath

It was great to be home for Christmas, but my visit was overshadowed by all the news of war. Most of my old friends from the Naval Reserve were already on active duty.

After the holidays, it was time for me to volunteer for the Navy, thereby avoiding the draft. I went to the armory and talked to the chief-in-charge. He said I could re-enlist as a chief because of my previous service. I passed the physical and it was agreed that I would be sworn in and shipped out the following week.

Mom and Dad drove me to the armory where we said our sad goodbyes.

I was one of a large group of men to be sworn in that day. On the way between rooms, I asked to see my papers.

"Sorry", the yeoman said, "I can't show them to you because you are going to be sworn in."

"Nothing doing", I replied, "I have the right to review them before I take the oath."

He sheepishly drew mine out of the group and handed it to me. Instead of being sworn in as a chief, I was going to be sworn in as a boatswain mate, a third class petty officer. I told the group to go ahead without me.

I went back to see the chief. He showed me a telegram he had received the previous week that read, "All former reservists would be re-enlisted at their former rate." I thought I could do better so I left the armory and arrived back home before my parents.

The Navy was organizing a Construction Battalion called Sea Bees. I went to their recruiting officer. He listed all of my experiences: dynamiting, surveying, construction, education, previous Navy service, etcetera and said I had enough experience to be a chief.

"How old are you", he asked.

"Going on 24", I answered.

He checked his book and said, "You have to be 28 to be a chief. I can enlist you as a third class petty officer."

I left the recruiting office.

Now my thoughts turned to Naval Air. I went to their recruiting office. I qualified in every way, even to having two years of college.

"What college did you attend?" the recruiting officer asked.

"Tulane"

What course did you take?"

"I had one year of general academics and one year of engineering."

"Sorry," he said, "You do not meet our requirement of two years of college. You need to have two years of general academics or two years of engineering."

That was the end of Naval Air.

Down the street was the recruiting office for the Army Air Corps. They gave me a mental exam, on which I scored very high. They gave me a physical, which I passed. They gave me the oath and I became an Aviation Cadet. They asked me if I could leave right away for Maxwell Field, Montgomery, Alabama. I asked for and was given three days to wind up my personal affairs - parties at home.

Three days later, they had more cadets than they could handle arriving at Maxwell Field. We were put into an old factory for processing and then trucked to Dothan, Alabama and put into "cold storage". We had physical training and drill twice a day for three months.

Back we went to Maxwell Field and a battery of tests. After passing all of them, I became an underclassman of the Class of 43A for flight training. We were the first class scheduled to graduate in 1943.

As underclassmen, we were treated the same as plebes at West Point and the Naval Academy. We marched to all formations, including meals, where more than a thousand of us, the entire Cadet Corps, sat down at one time. We had no liberty. Consequently, we were in better physical shape than our instructors.

In June, I was sent to Ocala, Florida with a group for Primary Flight Training. We flew Stearman PT-17s. It was a thrill to solo the first time, do a roll, fly upside down in an open cockpit and execute a perfect two-turn spin when on a check ride. As upperclassmen, we had liberty from Saturday noon till Sunday evening. We spent most of that time hanging out and swimming at Silver Springs.

We were sent to Shaw Field in Sumter, South Carolina for basic training. Besides more aerobatics, we learned formation flying, night flying, and cross-country navigation. We flew BT-13s.

Upon completion of basic training, we were given our choice of single or multi-engine advanced training, depending on whether we wanted to be fighter or bomber pilots. A group of us were put together, alphabetically - Rogers, Rose, Rudolph and Rummans - for training at Dothan, Alabama. We were always together throughout training. We all chose multi-engine. I figured I wanted more than one engine in case I lost one.

When I went to basic training, I was assigned a room in the barracks with a British Cadet from Wales and an American Cadet from Boston. My accent was a mix of Southern and Cajun, with a little Spanish thrown in, from living in New Orleans and Central America. We all spoke English but we could not understand what the other was saying because of our varied accents. Whenever one of us talked, the other two laughed.

From there, we went on to advanced training at Moody Field, Valdosta, Georgia. We flew twin engine Beechcraft AT-10s.

One evening, before Christmas, the Cadet Corps were trucked into Valdosta where we paraded and sang Christmas carols for the local citizens.

I had a couple of days off for Christmas, not enough time to go home, so I accepted an invitation to visit a girl in Dothan, Alabama whom I dated while there. The big Christmas dinner was at her grandmother's home. The grandmother didn't allow drinking in her house so, earlier that day, the local family members cleaned out the chicken coop, white washed it and set up the bar out there.

Graduation from flight training was in the middle of January, 1943. Only Rudolph's parents were able to attend the graduation ceremony. His mother pinned the gold bars and wings on those of us that had spent the year together.

The biggest thrill that day was getting my first salute.

Chapter Three

First Crew

My first assignment was four-engine transitions' training at Hendricks Field, Sebring, Florida. They had models B and C. We flew B-17s. These B-17s had no big stabilizers or armament. There were extra seats behind the pilot and copilot seats where the upper turret was eventually located.

In Sebring, I broke a finger on my right hand during a volleyball game. They took me off flying and gave me a couple of weeks leave. I was so proud to go home to New Orleans as an officer.

When I returned to Sebring, I was put back a class and shared a room with Robert Rosenthal from New York City.

Upon graduation from Sebring, we were shipped to Pyote, Texas. We had tar paper and wood shacks for barracks in the western Texas desert. HOT! They ran the base in three shifts daily. We had eight hours in ground school, eight hours on the flight line, and eight hours of rest. We changed shifts every week. It was impossible to sleep when our rest hours were from eight in the morning till four in the afternoon. The temperature in our barracks would get up to 120 degrees Fahrenheit. The only relief we could find was cold lemonade in the air-conditioned Officers' Club.

Once, while hanging out at the Officers' Club, I heard my name called. I looked around and didn't see anyone I knew. My name was called out again. I took another look and recognized no one. My name was called a third time. I looked up and was beginning to think I was hearing things. An officer got up and said, "You are Bill Rose from Panama". It was Jimmy, an old chum of mine from grammar school in Panama. We were in some of the same classes back in the '20s. The last time I had seen him was when I was in Panama with the Naval Reserve, summer of 1936 or 1937.

My first combat crew was formed in Pyote. Everyone assembled in a large room. Ten names, that comprised my first crew, were called out and told where to meet. On the way to meet my first crew members, the question went through my head, "Which one of these guys has a sister that I am going to marry?"

From Pyote, Texas we went to Dyersburg, Tennessee to continue training as a combat crew. Our liberty town was Memphis. Rosenthal's and my crew were always together. Our engineers, radiomen, gunners, bombardiers and navigators all trained together.

Upon completion of training at Dyersburg, I checked out my copilot as a first pilot. He was sent back to Pyote to train a new crew. I was assigned a copilot, Maxwell, who had just graduated from flight school and had his heart set on being a fighter pilot. Instead, he was assigned to our crew as copilot.

We were sent to Scott Field, Illinois to be processed for overseas and assigned a new B-17 to ferry across the ocean.

The day before our departure, I came down with a sore throat and was admitted to the hospital. The other crews flew off to England. My crew journeyed to St. Louis for liberty. They were the only crew left in the processing center and had the mess hall to themselves. They set up a schedule of one meal a day, at noon time, to consist of steak, eggs and ice cream. Everyday my crew would check with me as to my health and money supply before leaving for St. Louis, accompanied by the cooks.

After two weeks, my throat healed and my money ran out. Off we went in our brand new B-17 for England. It took us a week to get there.

We spent two freezing nights in Bangor, Maine, then three nights in Reykjavik, Iceland. We were then to fly to Prestwick, Scotland, but the weather got bad and we had to land at an emergency field on one of the Hebrides Islands. They weren't expecting us, nor were they expecting all of the other planes that landed there that evening. For supper that night we had our first taste of

English food, a slice of canned bully beef in hot milk made from powder. It was a rude awakening! We were glad the weather cleared the next day and we were able to deliver our plane to a depot in England. We were then trucked to Bovingdon.

Bovingdon was a Combat Crew Replacement Training School. We were instructed for two weeks, by combat veterans, on what to expect and how to evade if we were fortunate enough to land on the continent. We learned how to ditch the B-17 and the action of the Air Sea Rescue.

Upon completion of our training, we were assigned to the 92nd Bomb Group at Podington.

Our group was assigned to the 326th Squadron. I remember the squadron commander telling me, that if I could get by the first seven missions, I would have a chance of completing my tour of twenty-five missions. I asked him how many missions he had been on.

"Five", he replied.

He went down on his next mission.

Chapter Four

European Theater

My bombardier, Michelson, and navigator, Lewis, went on several combat training missions before we went as a crew. You can be sure we listened carefully to every word they said upon their return.

We were finally scheduled to go on our first mission as a crew. I flew as copilot with an experienced combat pilot. The target was Gdynia, Poland, East of Berlin. We flew across the North Sea, across Denmark, and across the Baltic Sea to get to the target. We returned the same route.

The Germans had moved a force of fighters up to Denmark and they were waiting for us on the return. We came under our first fighter attack. It was unbelievable to see a wall of tracers and a German fighter fly through them and shoot down a B-17. They were trying to kill me! The realization came over me that it was either them or me.

Our first mission's Daily Operations Journal noted the 62nd mission for the Eighth Air Force, 92nd Bombardment Group. It was 9 October 1943. The target was Gdynia, Poland. We took off at approximately 0815 hours. Gdynia was the longest flight in Flying Fortress history, to date, in the Eighth Air Force, an eleven hour flight. Flak was moderate and accurate. Twenty-five to thirty enemy single engine fighters were encountered. A crew went down near the Denmark coast, high hopes of the crew being safe as P/Ws. The downed crew was on their fifteenth mission.

After my first mission and debriefing, I returned to my nissen and found some letters on my bunk, left there by the orderly. One letter was from my radioman's sister, Marg.

Marg was the eldest of ten children from a small town, forty miles east of Pittsburgh, Pennsylvania. She had seven brothers and two sisters.

In late 1941, Marg was hired as society editor for the Latrobe Bulletin. She once wrote, "It was during the war years that my position at the paper changed considerably. There were some social events, but almost everything had an entirely different focus now. Many pages of the paper were devoted to pictures of local men who were in the service. There was a running column by a local woman, named Mrs. Smith, who corresponded with many young servicemen.

The most difficult time for me was the time of the Battle of the Bulge. During World War II, Latrobe had a group of soldiers, the National Guard Company M, that were involved in this battle. Many of them were young men with whom I had gone to high school.

During the war, the local Western Union telegraph office became swamped with telegrams of local casualties. It was my job to go to the Western Union office each morning to see what messages had come in. The telegrams relayed the news of soldiers, killed in action, wounded in action, and missing in action. I had to call on the families who had received the "killed in action" messages.

Needless to say, this was an ordeal. Even in their grief, families did respond to me, knowing that I had six brothers in the service. I was unable to eat or sleep, not knowing what the next day would bring. World War II was a war that every American fought, whether far away in a strange land or here at home in the U.S.A.

My family never put pen and paper away. We kept letters going all the time."

Marg, like Mrs. Smith from the newspaper, began to correspond with me after her brother, Frank, my radioman, sent a picture of our crew home in September 1943.

Marg's mother examined the picture and remarked, "Marg, I wish you would write a letter to this pilot and tell him we are offering our prayers for the safety of the crew."

"I was reluctant at first", Marg recalled, "but my mother persisted, and I wrote a friendly note to Lt. William Rose telling him of our concerns and offering our prayers for the crew."

Our second mission's Daily Operations Journal recorded the 63rd mission for the Eighth Air Force, 92nd Bombardment Group, 326th Squadron. It was 10 October 1943 and the primary target was Munster, Germany, with a secondary hit to Coesfeld, Germany. We took off just before noon that day. About twenty-five enemy planes were encountered, JU88s, FW190s and Me109s. It was considered a "Milk Run", as our group suffered very little damage due to flak and no planes were lost.

A few days later, I wrote back to Frank's sister.

October 13, 1943

Dear Marg,

Your letter was a pleasant surprise. I don't believe there is anyone who doesn't like to receive mail.

Yes, I always assume the responsibility of the crew when I am with them, but there is none to assume with our crew. All of the boys are really on the "beans".

Frank has really been doing a wonderful job on the radio. I can't tell you any of the circumstances because of censorship, but he has brought us safely in more than once. All I do is keep the plane flying in the direction he gives me. There are plenty of times I take the orders from him and I am real glad he is there and capable of passing them on to me, quick and correct.

If there is a long time between letters from him do not worry. We all work long and hard for days on end.

When we do get to bed, we just "flop". Once in a while we get a few hours off and that is when we get caught up on our correspondence.

Hoping to meet you soon, I remain

> Yours truly,
> Bill Rose

Chapter Five

"Black Thursday"

Our third mission was on 14 October 1943. The target was Schweinfurt, Germany. Ball bearing plants were to be hit today, in hopes of knocking out the manufacturing of German war machines. The weather was bad at take-off, it was raining and the field was covered in fog.

The 40th Combat Wing was composed of the 92nd Bomb Group, leading the mission, the 306th Bomb Group was the high group and the 305th Bomb Group was to be the low group to complete the box formation. The 305th

never got into position and it left the remaining two groups short of the 305th protective fire power. The Germans saw this and directed their attacks against us, rather than against the 41st Wing, which had all three of its groups flying in a tight formation. Consequently, the 305th suffered the fewest losses of this mission.

I flew in the No. 5 position, on the right wing of the second element leader of the 326th Squadron. Since we were the lead squadron, of the lead group, it was not difficult to hold our position during assembly or the rest of the mission.

Fighter strikes and air-to-air rockets were relentless as we penetrated deeper and deeper into Germany. One time my tail gunner, Eilers, called on the interphone that we were going to get relief as a formation of B-17s was coming up behind us. It should have been our low group which had never been in their proper position. Not five seconds later, he was on the interphone screaming, "Oh my God! They are German planes and they are firing rockets at us!" Just then a rocket went past my window and imbedded itself in the right wing of the second element leader. It did not take long for the fuel to ignite, the plane lost power, dropped back, and I believe some men bailed out before the plane blew apart.

The left wingman of our second element had been lost, previously, to enemy fire. I slid into the position of the second element leader. To hide in the sky, I moved our position forward, directly under the squadron leader's plane, so that his wingmen were protecting my flanks, too. To hold this position, I had to fly looking straight up through the top window.

Planes and parachutes were going down all around us. The thought went through my head, "what was the Air Force going to do when no planes, no men, returned from this mission?" I was not the only one that had this thought.

I had learned how to fly formation directly under the lead ship while training in Pyote, Texas, where our combat crews were formed and where we trained as a crew. One of my classmates was Robert Rosenthal, better known as "Rosie". When we arrived in Texas, the crews were formed alphabetically, so our bombardiers, navigators, engineers, radio operators and gunners had all been classmates in training. Consequently, our crews were close.

To teach our rookie copilots how to fly formations, and how to hand controls back and forth, Rosie and I took turns as the lead ship, while the others flew circles around the lead aircraft. We would start directly under the leader, drift to the left and come up passing wing tip to wing tip, slide over the top of the leader, descend down the other side passing wing tip to wing tip, again, and then slide under the leader to the starting position. What I learned in training I was now doing to save my plane and my crew. We were using every trick we could think of to take evasive action and still keep the formation together during horrific fighter attacks. We were scared! It seemed the fighter attacks would never let up until they shot us out of the sky.

During the battle, the ball turret got jammed. All that our gunner, Gay, could see were planes and parachutes going down, he was trapped and couldn't get out to use his chute if need be. We were under heavy fighter attack and every gunner was busy. No one could be spared to help him. I had to tell the crying man, "Get off the interphone. We will get to you as soon as we can." There were so many fighters attacking us.

I instructed my gunners to stop calling out attacks and to fire at will, their choice of targets, and to use short bursts to conserve ammunition. One time there was a German fighter coming in at us from the 9 o'clock level. I called to Kent, left waist gunner, to "get him". He, too, saw him coming straight at us but could only reply in a deep, frantic tone, "Don't bother me now, my gun is jammed."

After our formation turned on the Initial Point, start of the bomb run where we had to maintain a fixed air speed and altitude for the bombardier, bomb bay doors were going to be opened. I told my bombardier, Michelson, to let me know one minute before "bombs away" and I would drop back. He did, and the leader's bombs fell right in front of our nose.

After the bombing raid on Schweinfurt ended, we started heading home. The lack of fighter attacks on our return trip, over France, surprised us. I never figured out why the Germans stopped attacking us. Our ammunition was gone. Our oxygen was gone. We puffed on bailout bottles. We were tired. All of this made us an easy target.

Thank God the Germans spared us from anymore fighter attacks. Were they exhausted, too?

Then came England, covered with low clouds, fog, drizzle, practically no visibility, and darkness. The formation broke up over the channel. We entered the overcast and darkness trying to find a place to land. It was every pilot for himself.

I spotted outer perimeter lights of a field. The tower controller told me there was another plane on the lights, but he could not see either of us, he could only hear us. On the third pass I managed to land the plane.

Close to the end of the runway there was a jeep with a driver and another man, standing up in the jeep, holding a sign which read, "Follow Me". I tried the brakes. The brakes worked a little, but I could not slow down as much as I should have. I remember the guy, the one holding the sign, kicking and screaming at the driver to speed up and get out of the way, like he was spurring a horse in a race. I was afraid I was going to run them down. I had been through enough this day.

By the time I reached the end of the runway, I had slowed enough to turn the plane and keep it on the taxi strip and then into the first hardstand, parking area. Two engines had been turned off as soon as we touched down and the other two were cut as we swiveled around the hardstand. All of a sudden, everything was quiet. None of us could move. Did we really survive this day? Were we really safely on the ground?

We found out that we were at Bovingdon, the Combat Crew Replacement Center from which we had left three weeks earlier. An eternity had passed since our departure. Interrogation was by officers who had flown on the first Schweinfurt mission in August, and knew the horror we had been through.

The mess hall arranged supper for us but no one could eat, even though we were all starving. While we were playing with our food, the other crew, who had been in the pattern with us, who had given up trying to land, came into the mess hall. The pilot had climbed his plane up, set the automatic pilot to take the plane out over water, and the crew bailed out.

The night was miserable. Even though we were as tired as humans can get, we had trouble sleeping. I drank a few beers after supper and wished I had more as the night wore on. I did doze off a couple of times, but awoke with a jolt. Where was I?

Morning finally came. I took the crew out to the plane. We couldn't believe our eyes, holes everywhere! The plane looked like a sieve. Still, I had not lost a man, control, cable, engine or instrument. One of the guns in the ball turret had been hit and bent ninety degrees. It looked like it was going to shoot around the corner. Shell casings, belts, ammunition boxes, clothes, chunks of metal, Mae West life preservers, parachutes, harnesses, bailout bottles, etcetera, made the plane look like a trash dump.

I told the men to clean their guns, collect their gear, and straighten up the plane as much as possible. While we were doing this, an Air Corps General visited us. He said he was in the tower the previous night, while we were trying to land, and wanted to commend us on a superb job of flying. He said he was going to send commendations to the Eighth Air Force Headquarters for the entire crew, for our personnel records. That was the last we ever heard from him or his commendations.

That afternoon, the 92nd Bomb Group sent a plane to return us to our base at Podington. My radio operator, Frank, was missing. A search found him lecturing to the radiomen's class, telling them to listen to every word the instructors were saying because, "It is a hell of a lot worse!"

Many considered this mission the world's greatest one-day battle of World War II. Never before had there been an air battle with a higher percentage of losses on both sides, sixty of our crews, six hundred men, were known to have lost their lives this day.

The 92nd Bomb Group dispatched twenty-one aircraft, three aborted, and six were missing in action. Of the twelve which got back to England, only three landed at our base in Podington. Of the nine which came down at dispersed fields, throughout England, two crash-landed with one burning after a ground loop.

Chapter Six

Life after Schweinfurt

Nobody wanted to fly again. To get the crew back into the air, I got them to fly over to the Hundredth Bomb Group, to visit Rosie's crew. He had visited us to get his crew in the air after their rough mission, on which they were the only ones to return.

Our fourth mission was 3 November 1943. We were alerted early to prepare for the mission. The target was

Wilhelmshaven, Germany, take off was 0930. Visibility was poor and turbulence was rough. Twenty to thirty single engine fighters were encountered, no losses to Forts or crews. The Eighth Air Force did sustain light losses.

Our fifth mission was 5 November 1943. The target was Gelsenkirchen, Germany, in the Ruhr Valley. Take off was 1025. Five aircraft were lost from the Eighth Air Force.

NEWS

9 November 1943

Today all men participating in the last

Schweinfurt raid

were awarded Commendation Medals by the

British Prime Minister, Winston Churchill.

Our sixth mission was 1 December 1943. The target was Sieburg and Solingen, Germany. Take off was 0745. The mission averaged seven hours. Lack of flying equipment had reached a critical stage, lots of promises, no deliveries. Two Forts were damaged.

Our seventh mission was 16 December 1943. The target was Bremen, Germany. Our target area was a mass of smoke and flames. One plane mysteriously aborted inside enemy territory, with all engines operating. No update available on the plane or crew. After this mission, naval installations were practically knocked out of this war. The "Stars and Stripes" publicized the news of this raid and others of the Eighth Air Force.

Our eighth mission was 20 December 1943. The target was, once again, Bremen, Germany. Take off was 0820 hours. The target was hit and left burning. Flak was heavy and accurate.

December 21, 1943

Dear Marg:

Received your letter a few days ago, didn't answer it sooner because I spent all my spare time in bed trying to beat a cold. So far, so good, haven't missed a flight yet.

The whole crew is in good health and worrying about me because they don't want to fly with a strange pilot. I'm the same way, trying to keep in good health because I don't want to fly with a strange crew. No others work as smoothly as ours and each member of our crew has proven himself in tight places.

Frank is really a "busy bee" and doing a wonderful job. I just wish we could tell you of the wonderful things he has done. We depend on him more and more all the time. You can't brag enough about that brother of yours.

We won't have much of a holiday this year, but we all hope to be home next winter.

Good luck,
Bill Rose

Our ninth mission was 22 December 1943. The target was Osnabruck, Germany. Flak was light and inaccurate.

UPDATE
27 December 1943
Lt. Rose and crew received a newly assigned plane. Planes now have guns mounted at the waist windows and electronic superchargers.

Frank named our new plane, "Sky Scrapper". We had the ground crew put in additional armor plating behind and under the pilot and copilot seats. They put in additional large emergency oxygen bottles. They hid ammunition for us so we would have more than what was issued for each mission. We never ran out of ammunition again.

Our tenth mission was 30 December 1943. The target was Ludwigshaven, Germany. Take off was 0805. It was an eight hour flight with heavy cloud cover and turbulence. Two Forts aborted. One avoided a catastrophic landing when the tower alerted them that they did not have "wheels down". They were carrying a full bomb load.

Our eleventh mission was 31 December 1943. The target was Chateau Bernard, France. Take off was 0740. Our squadron was flying high in the low group. German long range fighter and bomber fields were hit. Our squadron averaged a ten hour flight. One aircraft and ten men were missing. Degree of success - bombs were seen to have hit hangars.

** Happy New Year 1944 **

Our twelfth mission was 4 January 1944. The target was Kiel, Germany. Take off was 0730. One pilot and crew unaccounted for. Eighth Air Force lost eighteen bombers and two escorting fighters.

Our thirteenth mission was 11 January 1944. The target was Oschersleben, Germany, center of German aircraft industry, one hundred and twenty miles from Berlin. Take off was 0855. Other targets for this day were Brunswick and Halberstadt, along with others near Berlin.

Little did the men know that today's mission would be one of those "stand out" days in the history of aerial warfare, similar to a second Schweinfurt. The "Forts" were engaged with a determined and aggressive bee hive of enemy fighters, all the way from the enemy coast line to their targets, and they had to fight their way out.

Our bomber crews met all types of German fighters. "Herman" was sending up everything that had wings on it and guns in it.

This was an epic air battle. There were many losses. At landing, the weather was overcast with a heavy drizzle of rain and snow – all landings were made at other bases.

One Fort was hit by flak in its right wing. The crew went down in flames on the pilot's twenty-fourth mission.

Our fourteenth mission was 14 January 1944. We did a short run, called a "Milk Run", to Linghem, France, in the Pas de Calais area. Take off was 1330. No losses for the Eighth Air Force.

NEWS

17 January 1944

Command of the Eighth Air Force and the Eighth Bomber Command are consolidated under one Command,

The Eighth Air Force

Head offices are now under the name of USSAFE,

United States Strategic Air Force in Europe.

A Major General is appointed as Commanding General

of the Eighth Air Force,

changing places with General Eaker.

Four Star General Eisenhower is the

Supreme Commander of Allied Forces in Europe

Our fifteenth mission was on 21 January 1944. The target was Bellevue, France. Take off was 1205. The trip averaged four hours No bombs were dropped.

Our sixteenth mission was on 29 January 1944. The target was Frankfurt, Germany. It was the first time the 92nd flew two groups. Take off was 0715. It was a bombing raid, but we also dropped "chaff", tin foil strips, to throw off the radar sightings of the anti-aircraft guns, it was fairly effective. No losses to fighters.

Other Eighth Air Force units lost a total of twenty-nine bombers, five fighters. Enemy losses estimated to be one hundred and two fighters.

Our seventeenth mission was 30 January 1944. The target was Brunswick, Germany. Take off was 0830. We encountered thirty to forty fighters. Flak was moderate to accurate. No losses to 326th Squadron. Twenty-five heavies and five fighters were lost.

Two B-17s collided as they were climbing out through the overcast. Both ships went down.

On one of our missions, a German fighter pilot put a 20mm shell in our cockpit from a tail attack. The shell knocked out our oxygen system, ricocheted off the armor plating behind the copilot, went through Gurke's (our engineer) leg and spent itself by cutting the rubber holding my chest type chute so that it opened. It was chaos for a minute, but we stayed in formation. I had to get on emergency oxygen, assess the battle damage and get help for Gurke, while still flying the plane in formation, as the group was still under fighter attack.

I don't remember how many times I lost one engine due to flak or mechanical trouble. One time we lost number three engine which had the cockpit heater. We were really cold! Every particle of moisture from our breath froze and collected on the window overhead. On the way home, I collected it, made a snow ball and threw it at the copilot.

Flying combat was taking a physical toll on us, even though we were beginning to have more and longer fighter protection on our missions. After about seventeen missions, the crew was sent to a rest home in southwest England for a week. I think I slept day and night for the week. We were treated like we were the owners of the estate. Back at the base, I had started taking pills to sleep the nights before a mission and pills to wake me up the next morning. The Squadron Flight

Surgeon kept a sharp eye on the combat crews and helped us get through our missions.

February 14, 1944

Howdy Marg:

Glad to receive your air-mail this afternoon. Find me anyone, anyplace, who doesn't like to receive mail.

Sorry to hear you worried about us after the news of our mission on January eleventh. Worrying doesn't do anyone any good. If something does happen to us, we will get out alive and it might take months for word of our good health to get to you. Never give up hope, but at the same time, don't think about it. With the experience we now have, and with only a few missions remaining, there is little chance of anything getting us. They had their chance and missed.

If the plane is at all flyable, she will bring us back to England. Frank is going to have some good stories to tell you when he gets back. He might color them a bit but they will probably be based on facts.

I've got a couple of good stories on Frank's fine work.

Returning from a mission, one afternoon, we were an hour late and ran into bad weather. I had Frank call the base on his radio for a censored reason. Come to find out, none of the planes had returned or transmitted any messages till the time Frank called. They had imagined all sorts of horrible things happening, but as soon as they heard the radio, they knew everything was all right. I received quite a few compliments and passed them on to where they were due.

The other story concerns our ex-navigator, Lewis. He has been taken off the crew and does special work. Consequently, he flies with quite a few crews. He told me the other night, that out of all the radio operators he has flown with, none of them were as good as Frank. He should know.

Frank has probably written all about the rest home. It was really wonderful. A few days before going we didn't fly and we haven't flown since. The vacation has done wonders for all of us. The whole crew is a lot peppier and a little bit on the "eager" side. Everyone is in the best of health and enjoying themselves.

The rest home we stayed at was photographed by "LIFE" and they ran the pictures and article last year. I think it was in the summer.

If the weather is cold enough to form ice, it is too cold for me. I have never been ice skating or sledding. I plan to try them some day, but not for long. The good old tropics are the place for me.

Frank didn't tell me his brother had been accepted for cadet training. Even though we have been together nine months, we never talk about the families, unless it is a bit of praise, or trouble, and then I try to help out. That's one of the things I learned back in peace times, when I was studying for a commission in the Navy as an enlisted man. Practically all of our instructors were Annapolis graduates.

They poured into our heads to "be friendly but not familiar". By remembering that all the time, and getting rough with the boys once in a while, I think it helped shape the best crew that ever came across, and is keeping it the best crew in the European Operational Theater. As soon as I finish, I am going to order them all out and try to get them to let their hair down. We are going to have one rip-roaring good time.

This seems to bring everything up to date and so I will close till later.

                              Regards,
                              Bill

Our eighteenth mission was on 20 February 1944. The target was Leipzig, Germany. No squadron notes for this mission.

Our nineteenth mission was on 22 February 1944. It was a flight to Aalborg, Denmark. Take off was 0805 in a light snow flurry. Our squadron was leading the wing today. This was more or less a diversionary mission so that a large bomber force could go deep into Germany to bomb aircraft factories. Flight time was over eight and one half hours. One Fort was lost due to enemy fighter action.

Our twentieth mission was on 28 February 1944. The target was Harbaville, France, in the Pas de Calais region. We were targeting ground installations. Four or five Forts were damaged. Allied forces lost two hundred twenty-three bombers and thirty-nine long-range fighters.

* Bombing this month was directed against the Luftwaffe*

Our twenty-first mission was on 3 March 1944. The target was Berlin, Germany. The boys were briefed for Capital "B" formations. Cloud cover was high. Bombs were jettisoned into the channel, "A lot of fish were killed today."

Our twenty-second mission was on 4 March 1944. The target was Bonn, Germany. Take off was 0830. Our crew drew the low, low spots. It was a six and one half hour flight. Cloud cover made visual sighting impossible.

Our twenty-third mission was on 6 March 1944. The target today was "Big Berlin". Take off was 0800. Flak took down one plane and crew, not known if they bailed out. Enemy opposition consisted of Me109s, FW190s, and JU88s. Heavy to intense flak was accurate. One Fort carried the 500 lb. incendiaries, the first time this new weapon was used.

The Eighth Air Force lost sixty-eight heavies, eleven fighters and six hundred and eighty men.

Our twenty-fourth mission was on 8 March 1944. The target was Erkner, a section of Berlin. Take off was 0800. A ball bearing plant was the target hit today.

Our twenty-fifth mission was on 20 March 1944. The target was Frankfurt, Germany. Take off was 0810. The weather was bad. The estimated flight time was seven hours and forty-five minutes. No bombs were dropped. Flak was light and inaccurate. No enemy fighters were encountered.

We finished our tour and kissed the ground when we got out of the plane that day. The enlisted men on the crew had flown the same twenty-five missions I had and we were fortunate that only one, Gurke, had been wounded.

My biggest worry, during this tour, was that one of my crew members would be killed. I did not pal around with them because I felt if anything horrible happened I would have to continue on and I didn't know if I would be able to handle that. They were counting on me to get them back home.

If I had not been put back a class at Sebring, because of my broken finger, and put in the hospital at Scott Field, I would have arrived in England about a month earlier. Would I have been able to survive twenty-five missions then?

We were each handed a Distinguished Flying Cross, for surviving, and then shipped home by troop transport.

Chapter Seven

Back in the States

As the ship passed the Statue of Liberty at dawn, we were escorted by a fire tug with all its pumps spraying water in the air, and another boat with the song, "God Bless America", being played through its loud speakers. It was a very touching homecoming!

This was before the invasion. Everyone was still headed overseas. Very few men were returning. I would have stuck it out till the end of the war. Failure of communication sure changed my life.

May 28, 1944

Howdy Marg:

Pardon the paper but I have none at all and the PX is closed. Usually when I use the Red Cross paper it is because I am in the hospital, but this time I am in paradise.

All of my mail from overseas caught up with me down here the other day and one of the letters was yours written on March second. You had such good clippings in it plus some jokes at the end.

Well, I might not have the jokes but enclosed is a clipping the folks saved for me. I don't keep a scrap book so I am passing it on.

I don't know if Frank told you all about the Brunswick raid or not, but the only thing they left out of the newspaper was that twenty-four hours later we were still sweating and freezing at the same time.

I imagine you have told Frank you wrote to me a couple of times while we were in England. Send the article on to him when you have finished with it. Also, tell him I am waiting for the prints of the pictures which he promised me, which is practically a print of every picture he took. If you want, just pass this whole letter along.

I plan to visit him as soon as I get to my next station. At the present time I am enjoying life, as Frank is probably doing the same in Atlantic City. Tell him Kent is in the hospital at Coral Gables for a minor operation. Lewis and Gay have finished their tours and are on their way home.

How did you enjoy having Frank home again? Did you think he had changed since his last visit?

Believe it or not, but I didn't want to tell any of the fellows "goodbye" when we left New York. It sure was a lot easier to break up the crew that way, especially ours. We thought too much of each other. It paid dividends, too.

It sure feels funny not to have the fellows around, especially while on leave. I believe all of us would have enjoyed it more if we could have been sent together to the same rest home at the same time.

I have to hand it to the Air Corps for treating their returnees better than men in any other branch of the service. All of us are enjoying vacations none of us ever thought possible, not even in peace time. This last week proved to me that what I was doing was the way to fight a war, and such carousing around as I am doing; at least no one gets hurt.

Marg, I want to get out a few more letters tonight and so I will bring this to a close till a later day.

For this marvelous country,

Bill

Article enclosed:

The Times Picayune

New Orleans, LA

Tuesday, April 11, 1944

**FIGHTERS ESCORT
LAME FORT BACK**

Orleans Pilot Tells of Air
Rescue Over Reich

A New Orleans Flying Fortress pilot and his crew will continue to do their part in the bombing of Germany due to the aid of two unknown Mustang pilots who escorted the Fortress, "Black Magic", 500 miles back safely after it fell out of formation 15 miles from Berlin, according to a dispatch from the Eighth Army Air Force bomber base in

England. The pilot was First Lieutenant William B. Rose son of Mr. and Mrs. P.C. Rose ...

Three of "Black Magic's" engines started acting up just before the Fort made its run on the target and the plane could not keep up with the formation. After Lieutenant Rose ordered the bombardier to drop his bombs and lighten the plane, "Black Magic" was still not able to catch up with the formation.

Lieutenant Rose was faced with the decision of crash landing and he and his crew becoming prisoners or trying to fly back to England alone with the possibility of being shot down. He headed for home, counting on the help of the Mustang and Lightning fighter pilots.

"Just as we turned around we flew through a formation of Lightings headed for Berlin", said Lieutenant Rose after returning safely to his base. "Just as they passed us two Me109s, just out of range, began maneuvering to attack us. Our Fortress was just a gleam in the eyes of those two Jerry pilots when that Lightning outfit took out after them. Four of those twin-tailed P-38s chased those two Nazis right down to the deck and out of sight before they headed on toward Berlin to give our bombers cover over the target."

After flying on for about 15 minutes, two P-51 Mustangs saw the Fortress and came to its aid. Lieutenant Rose said, "one of them came in close on our wing and motioned to his oxygen mask and then pointed down," he went on "I finally realized he was trying to tell me he was almost out of oxygen so I went down to about 12,000 feet. Then those two Mustangs stuck with us all the way across enemy territory and halfway out over the Channel."

Knowing they were safe from enemy fighters and knowing the Mustangs would be leaving them; Lieutenant Rose called over the radio, saying "Ten men owe their lives to you fellows. Much obliged." One of them called back, "don't mention it. That's our job, we're only too glad to help."

From Lockbourne Army Air Base, Columbus, Ohio:

June, 7, 1944

Howdy Marg:

Your letter has flown all over the country and finally caught up with me here this afternoon.

I really got a big kick out of the article you sent. Frank told me on the boat coming back that he was really going to tell some stories and he sure did paint them up, but what he said is based on actual facts.

Marg, will you please send this on to Frank when you finish. I can see no sense in writing him when I can carry on a correspondence with a sweet thing.

Glad to hear you made another rest home, goldbricker. If there is anyone that is going to keep out of the army it's you. If it is as nice as the stories I have heard of the place, you will be there for the duration plus six. Don't blame you for taking all you can get. I'm really jealous. Got as fat as a little pig while home and now look so healthy they put me back to work.

Just got up here Monday night and am starting to fly tomorrow morning at five. Of all the ungodly hours, that's it.

They are putting a bunch of us thru an instructors' course which lasts from six to nine weeks. It's exactly the same thing I had at Sebring before I picked up the bunch of bums at Pyote.

The chow, field and everything about this place is really wonderful. Guess I haven't gotten used to the luxuries here in the States yet. After spending six weeks in the heat down South, sleeping under blankets sure feels good. Believe it or not, but this is the first time I have ever been in the North, except for one short visit in 1939.

When we finish our course here they might keep me as an instructor, but will probably send me out. It sure would be great to stay up here till October or November and then be sent south for the winter.

Marg, if you see a B-17 flying circles around the town soon it will probably be me, that is, if I can find Latrobe on the map. I haven't looked for it yet. We might even try to get low enough to read the street signs and pick out the house.

Glad to hear you are planning a nice vacation to New York City. Yep, I think it is a wonderful town. There is more to do there than you'll ever get around to. I only spent the same two days Frank did - and boy - that's the town for me. Haven't been into Columbus, but from the stories I hear, it has nothing wrong with it.

There's nothing like a vacation away from everybody - just bumming around is a nice way of saying it. Those two weeks at Miami Beach served me just as good as your trip to New York City will for you.

Well, Marg and Frank, this just about winds things up for this evening. Be sure each of you drops a line when you get the chance.

I'll write you a separate letter, Frank, as soon as I get an address.

Loafing,
Bill

Chapter Eight

Invitation

June 19, 1944

Howdy Marg:

I received your letter and the invitation. As soon as I got my orders to come up here I thought I might be able to get over to Latrobe and meet Frank's family.

It will be impossible for me to come over the weekend of July first. I have to fly that Saturday afternoon and Sunday morning, and then, I have to go to ground school Sunday afternoon. That's more than I can get off from.

I should be finished with ground school around the tenth of July and finished flying shortly thereafter. We should have a couple of days off before shipping out. As soon as I get enough time off I want to come over, even if it is the middle of the week. You might be away on vacation, but I will probably drop over anyway. I'll send a telegram first, but it would be easier if you sent me a phone number, and then I could reach you anytime and we could probably arrange a trip quicker.

There had better not be any fuss or frills when I get over. I've been living in these barracks too long. I just want to get to a home, take off my tie, roll up my shirt sleeves, put my feet under a table, and relax. Whenever I get tired of that, I will just roll around on the floor and absorb a little of that good old home atmosphere.

No, Marg, I haven't flown over Latrobe yet. Plan to do it the first opportunity. I got over Pittsburgh the other night and then had to turn around and come back. I'll fly over the house now that I know where it is. I had planned on coming right down and reading the street signs and number, but it won't be necessary now. Think I'll find it okay.

I've only been in to Columbus twice. It seemed to be very nice with plenty to do. They are keeping me too busy out here at the field. Can't learn the town the way I'd like to.

They are giving me the same course I had at Sebring over again, so that I will be able to teach the way all the other instructors are teaching the new boys to handle the airplane. Also, they are teaching us how to handle new pilots and "the bones they pull" and what we should look out for. I'd much rather train combat crews and hope that is what I get. I sure do miss our crew.

Well, Marg, I'm going to close for the time being and will drop you another line shortly.

Ex-boss man

Bill

July 12, 1944

Howdy Marg:

I finished up the instructors' course here Monday afternoon and tried to get a couple of days off to get over to Latrobe. The commanding officer said "nothing doing". There are no orders for me yet and as soon as someone figures out what to do with me he wants to ship me right on out. Now I am enjoying another vacation, except that I have to check in at headquarters twice a day to see if anything comes in.

If they keep me here I'll get over the first weekend possible, but if they ship me out, I probably won't be able to make the visit this trip. Anyway, whatever comes up, I will give you a phone call.

The last couple of nights a group of us have been bumming around town. There are very few nice places to go in town. There isn't even a night club in town. They are on the outskirts. It takes a fortune to get there in a cab, and from what I know, none of them are very good, and what floor shows there are, they are terrible. This is quite a bit different from New York City.

I got your post card from New York City. It sure did bring back some fine memories and made me wish I was there. That's the place for me.

I never did get to fly over Latrobe, Marg. Several times we got close by but it was just a little too far out from our flight plans. They really make us keep on course and on time now that there are so many planes.

There is nothing much new around here. I haven't heard from any of the fellows lately, because I have failed to answer their last letters. Therefore, I'm going to cut this short and try to get in some more notes tonight.

Give my regards to all.

Bill

July 23, 1944

Howdy Marg:

They have kept me as an instructor against my wishes. It is not the place but the work and all the flying that gets me. Combat was easy compared to this, but they shoot at you over there. We didn't mind that too much, but we certainly didn't like being hit.

Right now it looks as if I will be able to get over to Latrobe this coming weekend. I fly Saturday morning and then I'm off till the following Monday noon. I am going to try to fly over Saturday afternoon, but will probably have to come by train, which means I won't be there till later Saturday night. Anyway, I'll let you know when and how I will arrive if all of you folks will be home. If everyone is away this weekend, I will make it some other time because I will be here a long time now and will be able to get over anytime it suits you.

I sure did enjoy your long letter, Marg, and was glad to hear you had such a marvelous time in New York City. I sure would like to have a vacation and spend it in that city. Thanks for the autographed post card.

The story about Frank was good. I just had a short letter from him the other day and he said he had broadcasted over a local station. A record of the broadcast was made. I sure would like to hear it.

When we came back from the Schweinfurt raid, last October, we made an emergency landing at the same school we went thru before being assigned in England. The next morning I rounded up the crew to go out to the plane and clean it up. Everybody was around except Frank. He was in the same classroom where he had been taught, but instead of being there as a student, he was lecturing to the new class, telling them all about combat. He had only been out of school three weeks and had only been on three missions. The way he talks makes me think Frank has a great future in politics.

Well, I'll wind this up now. Hope to meet you and the rest of the family that are home on Saturday.

Bill

An invitation from Marg to visit her, her family, and Frank's friends, was the high spot of my assignment at Columbus. She said she would meet me at the Pittsburgh train station.

When I got off the train in Pittsburgh, no beautiful girl rushed up to meet me. I started asking all the "good lookers" if they were Marg.

"No."

The crowd dispersed and I was left alone, afraid to ask the few remaining girls if one of them was Marg.

I went to the Station Master's office and asked him to page Marg on the loud speakers. She arrived with her dad and brother. They had arrived late and had just entered the station when they heard the page. We drove to Latrobe, stopping for a beer and a chance to talk and get acquainted.

After arriving at their home, meeting her mother and the rest of the family, we went out. We visited the bars to meet Frank's friends. The party lasted till after five in the morning. Marg was wearing an engagement ring. I was on my best behavior for the whole weekend.

August 1, 1944

Howdy Folks,

Just a note of appreciation and to let you know I got home okay. The train wasn't too crowded and I had a seat in an air-conditioned coach. The trip really went fast, as I fell asleep for a couple of hours, I am Frank's close second on "sack time".

Mrs. Cline, everything was wonderful and the home cooking sure did taste good. They won't be able to keep me here if there is enough time off to get to Latrobe, and then, you won't be able to keep me out of the kitchen.

Thanks a lot for the beer and the car, Mr. Cline. It sure was a pleasure to ride and drive once more, and then, top it all off with a tall, cool drink. That topped off the best weekend I have spent in a long time.

Sorry I missed you on the goodbyes, Donald, but I'll be back shortly and tell you goodbye twice the next time I leave.

It sure was swell to go out with you and your friends, Marg. I'm looking forward to when we can all bum around again. Tell all the boys and girls "hello" for me and I hope to see them all again. Saturday night was the most enjoyable one I have spent since being back in these good old States.

When I got back here there was a letter from Michelson, our bombardier, waiting for me. He is still in combat but hopes to join us on this side of the ocean soon. He has received the Distinguished Flying Cross with an oak leaf cluster plus a couple of letters of commendation on the targets he has hit. He has also qualified to be a navigator, and has obtained that rating.

Our ex-plane, "Sky Scrapper", that Frank named, has completed over fifty missions and is still going strong.

I have also received a letter from Lewis, our navigator. He is instructing navigators at Rapid City, South Dakota and he hates it. With the experiences we have had, all students seem dumb. It is hard to realize that we were once the same way.

If I write anymore, this will cease to be a note. Anyway, that's one excuse for closing.

Regards to all,
Bill

Bill kept very few articles and letters but here is one letter he kept from Marg:

August 6, 1944

Dear Bill:

Just sittin' here wishin' this could be last weekend!

I want you to know that last Saturday night I had one of the best times I've ever had in my life. It wasn't what we did, but the fact that you were such a "down-to-earth", regular fellow that made it that way.

You were as good as a tonic for mom and dad. They've talked about you all week. Your personality really registered with all of the folks you met during your short visit here.

Enclosed are the pictures. It was such fun taking them –wasn't it? They turned out pretty well, for being snapped at random. A few did not come out well – too much light.

Frank's recording has arrived in Greensburg and is to be played over Station WHJB (620 kilocycles) at 2:15 on Friday afternoon, August eleventh. We'll hear it here at the house after my dear brother has had his say "on the air".

This has been a hectic week. There was a large benefit party – people came from miles around to attend it. Dad won $50.00 on the horse races they held at the party. Then there was the opening of the new hospital and I was a receptionist – it was fun and I saw people I don't see real often. Then at the house we've had company from West Virginia and Boston and to top off all that, I've been a little perplexed, yet relieved, - because - I've broken my engagement.

We heard from Frank on Monday, he wondered if you had arrived. While we were having fun – he was sweating out a good sore throat – he had his tonsils removed. He hasn't said anything more about a definite furlough date – but we're hoping it's soon.

Learning to know a person in a few hours was a new experience for me, Bill, but I feel as tho' I've known you for ages. Each and every one of us wants you to come back soon – if you enjoyed being here you can prove it by coming again any free time that you might have.

Frank's sis –
"Marg"

Chapter Nine

Lockbourne

From Lockbourne Air Base in Columbus, Ohio

August 13, 1944

Howdy Marg:

It sure was good to hear from you and look at the pictures- they're marvelous. It seems as if I can't get my fill of 'em.

Did you send a set to Frank? I haven't heard from him for a couple of weeks and am imagining they are moving him some place. Hope he gets home and lets me know when because I will do my best to get back over while he is there. Maybe they will let me skip a few classes and flying periods. If they don't, I will miss them anyway.

I really want to visit Latrobe every chance possible, but it isn't next door. Also, my father's family comes from around Detroit and I have to pay them a visit the first time there is enough legitimate time-off.

It sure is hot here in the room tonight. This place is usually nice and cool till about four in the evening, and then it is hot till the night winds blow, around eleven, which makes me sleep under covers. It is not as nice as Latrobe and I doubt if I will ever find a place I like as well.

It is easy to visualize you writing on a Sunday afternoon and wishing it was another. All of my Sundays in Columbus are that way. I have never seen a post and town that closes up like this place. We can't fly and in town only a very few restaurants are open and it is very difficult to find even three point two beer. Therefore, I spend my days here on the post drinking rum and Coke and having a good time writing letters, doing odds and ends, then going to a show and reading till I fall asleep. It is really very lonely.

I have gotten tired of hanging around and just doing nothing all the time. Tomorrow I don't fly till eight at night and so I am going shopping for a car. With one, it will be possible to go out to the golf course, lake, and to town. Also, if enough gas can be saved, I will be able to drive to Latrobe once in awhile.

    Thanks, Marg, for all the pretty compliments in your letter. It was just swell being "home" again because, even though I had never seen any of you in pictures, or knew anything about the family, I just felt like I knew all of you from your letters and from working with Frank. None of you felt like strangers to me. I wanted to kiss your Mom goodbye, and I think she wanted to do the same, but there were just too many people around and she was just about crying when I left. Besides, I am bashful.

    The station that broadcasted Frank's "spiel" is just a little too far under-powered to reach here. I'll be back shortly and if you have the recording we will find a place to play it. Then I will let you in on the secret of how much is really the truth.

    It is hard to see how you had a hectic week if Mr. Cline won $50.00 on the horse races at the benefit party. After all, benefit parties have to benefit someone and it might as well be your father as the next man. The horses are running here in Columbus now and I will pay them a visit if I get a car. I won't win anything, used up all my luck over Germany.

Surprised to hear you broke your engagement. Even though you never said anything about it, I couldn't help but hear some of the girls make remarks when we were all out together. I never paid any attention to them and can only recollect one remark now. I can't imagine how you feel because I have never been engaged.

Of course you felt as if you had known me for ages. One of the best ways to get to know a person is by the letters he writes and we have written quite a few.

It sure was swell to meet you personally, Marg, and I hope we can have lots of more good times together.

Tell the family "hello" for me.

Since you aren't engaged anymore, I can sign this letter as I do all of mine.

Love,
Bill

August 20, 1944

Howdy Marg:

It sure was swell to receive that nice big letter from you and all the latest news.

Since Frank has been sent to rehabilitation in Miami, I doubt if he will get home. They usually ship their men straight to the new assignments. Once he gets there they might give him a furlough. Here's hoping he gets what he wants, but I doubt it. If he asks for Texas, or someplace in the South, he will be sent north. The army is still up to its old tricks.

Your description of Frank's recording tallied with what he wrote. The record, "My Mama Done Told Me", was a good one to play before the speech. They should have played it before Frank talked in St. Pete. Maybe he wouldn't have had as much to say.

I got a big kick at what I saw while looking out my window this afternoon. A dump truck went by with several prisoners in it. On top of the cab sat the guard just talking away and using both hands for emphasis. One of the prisoners had the rifle.

Your weekend at the mountain lodge sounded marvelous. I just wish there was something around here like that. There is absolutely nothing that stirs here on Sundays, except a few swimming pools. These days really get me down. I usually bum around town Saturday nights, sleep till noon on Sundays, and then write, read, go to the show, and drink myself silly. I have asked the few other single fellows what they do all day, but none of them seem to know, except that they will away the time somehow. Anyway it sure is lonesome.

All my spare time last week was spent looking at cars. The one I really want, the dealer won't part with. I'm going to keep on looking. Maybe something will turn up. Anyway, it gives me something to do, and the walking doesn't hurt.

I sure wish I was spending the week at Tudor Manor with Joan and Deedee. Golly, why can't I be young like them and spend the summer playing? Too bad they didn't build this school right by Latrobe. It sure would be a lot nicer. I really envy all of you.

This coming week, I'm flying to New York with all my students. We are leaving Wednesday night and will fly ten hours non-stop and land at West Point. We will then go to the big city and gallivant around for twenty-four hours, after which, we will fly directly back. This will put us over Latrobe at about three o'clock Friday afternoon. If you see a "Fort" circling around there, making a lot of noise, you can blame it on me. Don't be taking a siesta or you will be woken up. It's no fair sleeping at your desk, anyway.

After spending all my life in the South, I will never spend another summer there. Never knew they made such cool weather in August.

Well, Marg, guess I'll close for lack of more to write about. Tell all the folks "hello" for me and tell Frank, when you write to him, to be sure to answer that big letter I wrote.

I also heard from <u>Captain</u> Michelson. He has finished his tour, plus extra missions, and has now volunteered for more.

Love,
Bill

August 27, 1944

Howdy Marg:

Guess you know by now I didn't fly over Latrobe Friday afternoon. Sorry to have made you look outside so often. I did go by there at four-ten this morning but didn't make any noise. It would have been a shame to wake you up and then not see you.

There is a reason we didn't make it on schedule. The trip up was uneventful, long and tiring. We went via

Louisville, Chattanooga, Nashville, Atlanta, Greensborough, Richmond and Harrisburg.

When we landed at West Point, I found we had a broken wheel rim that had chewed the casing and we can't figure out why the tire didn't blow on landing. Now I am concerned I have used up the last of that Rose's luck.

It took me till noon to make arrangements for another wheel assembly, after which, we all went to the big city. I got a room at the Roosevelt, ate a big meal and just passed out, but first managed to send a telegram to friends of mine who live on Staten Island.

They claimed my phone rang for five minutes at six o'clock with no answer, but when they called again at nine, they managed to get me up. I went on out to their apartment.

Come to find out, the husband, Johnny, was at sea but his sister was there on vacation and also a newly married couple. The guy was a fellow I had bummed around with in high school and a few years afterwards. We were shipmates in the Naval Reserve. He is now a lieutenant in the Coast Guard and had just returned from eighteen months of Foreign Service. The five of us talked for four hours. It made me feel good.

When we got back to Stewart Field, Friday afternoon, I found my troubles had only begun. They had shipped us the wrong inner tube and ours couldn't be used because of a high pressure leak. It took me until ten that night to find out there wasn't one like we needed in the area and had to make arrangements to have one flown to us from Lockbourne.

They got the tube up to us Saturday evening and it took till one in the morning to get the plane in shape to fly. Rather than sleep for a few hours, then fly and run into bad weather, I decided to fly on home and spend quite a few hours in the "sack" while it rained, which is exactly what I did all day.

I had the snapshots with me that we took on my visit. They sure did like them. Johnny's sister pointed to one of them and wanted to know who the guy was. It was me.

Those pictures you sent of Frank in St. Pete are really good. He sure looks fine and in the best of health.

It sure surprised me to know that something you see can move you to tears. I am that way, too. A good play, show, scene or anything can affect me. If they don't, I think they're lousy. Usually a good thing will make me completely forget my surroundings.

No, I don't think Michelson is doing anything daring or is "flak happy". He is just quiet, cool and knows what he is doing. Our tour didn't affect him in any way. Frank did lose his appetite, weight and became nervous; Kent almost had a complete nervous break-down; I lost about fifteen pounds in weight and gave other signs of strain. I could go on that way about each crew member. That's why Michelson is still over there and I have now volunteered to go back. The reason I want to go is because I am so lonesome and out of place here. My papers go in at the end of this month and I should hear something, one way or another, by the end of September.

This past week I have received letters from Frank, Eilers and Gay. It was the first Gay had written. He has gotten married and is now stationed in Galveston, Texas going thru a radio school. Frank's letter was from Maine and I guess you might have his new address by now.

The first part of the week I spent shopping for a car. I found a '41 Chevy that had been in storage and is in fine condition. I drove it for a day and decided to buy it. The engine is in perfect condition. There are several minor things that needed to be done and so I left it in the garage during my sojourn to New York. It might help these Sunday blues, but talking to you, or listening, would be a sure cure. If you can't make it on the weekend, I will stir up the blues on any day of the week you desire. Monday is usually an excellent day.

The paratrooper that is assigned to Lockbourne instructs students going thru here. They might give us a course in jumping later on. It would be my second.

It seems I am more of a rambler when it comes to writing than you are, Marg. I even stopped and took my girl to the show. We saw Kay Hepburn in "Dragon Seed" or something. It was only fair.

Thanks a lot for the pictures and I might remember to put them in the envelope before it is sealed. If not, they will be along in the next letter.

Tell all the folks "hello" for me.

                        Love,

                        Bill

                    September 4, 1944

Howdy Marg:

The big news of the past week was a visit by Lewis. He landed at an airport close by and spent the night in

Columbus. We bent our elbows and really had a good bull-session.

Frank and Lewis are having a big time in Rapid City. They seem to have all their nights off. Lewis has a car and so to town the two of 'em go.

Besides that, the War Department General Order number (Censored) gives an account of the first division's actions on the Brunswick raid of January eleventh. As soon as our personal orders come thru, all of us on that mission will wear the presidential citation, a blue rectangular ribbon lined with gold around the border. It is worn over the right pocket.

I received a letter from Michelson today, said he had also heard of it and he is now expecting another citation, which will give him an oak leaf cluster to go with it. Also, he heard Maxwell, our former copilot, is a prisoner of war.

Michelson has received the fourth oak leaf cluster to go with his air medal and his second letter of commendation from General Williams. He now has about forty-five missions to his credit, with the last one to "happy valley", the Ruhr, which was very rough. He also mentioned that "Sky Scrapper" now has sixty-two missions to her credit and will soon be retired from combat.

Also, I had a letter from Gay, our ball turret gunner and radio operator (or did I write this before?). Anyway, he is married and going to a radio school in Galveston, Texas.

As for me, I graduated my first batch of students and have been taking things easy. I did a hundred odd things that I have kept putting off and then went over to Buckeye Lake to see my girl on Saturday and Sunday. Today I just slept and tomorrow night we start to work on some new "Luftwaffe Bait" (students).

Besides this, my brother, who is only eighteen and a torpedo man in the Navy, is coming for a visit in the morning. I have only seen him once since 1939. That was at Christmas in '41.

Lewis said he raised Cain with Frank for never telling him he had such a swell sister. I showed him the picture and he said he will put Frank in a "brace", exaggerated position of attention, for about half an hour on his return.

Tell all the good people "hello" for me and I will be back up that way as soon as possible.

Love,
Bill

Chapter Ten

Accidents

From my family's home in New Orleans:

October 2, 1944

Howdy Marg:

Please excuse the long period of silence from me, but I had a series of three accidents, none serious, but they left me shaking and scared.

The first, I believe, I wrote you about. It was the trip to New York, when we had the broken wheel.

The second came while flying my kid brother to Harrisburg, Pennsylvania. Five minutes before landing, number four engine became covered with oil and scared us. We landed okay, with no fire, but had to remain overnight to get the prop changed.

When we flew back the following day, we flew right over Latrobe and I circled awhile, but couldn't get down low because of the heavy air traffic and clouds. Nevertheless, I could pick out your office, church, school, and home. It sure did look good and I was wishing I was on the ground there.

The third accident came the following weekend. While I was demonstrating "close-ins" to the new students, the plane got away from me, when about fifty feet in the air. She dropped in on the front wheels and the left one broke. I don't know why I let it happen. The plane rolled merrily on down the runway on the one good wheel; till it was going so slow there was no more holding it. The plane then did an easy "ground loop" to the left. All the switches had been cut and nothing caught fire.

The colonel and I had a big argument about it. It all boiled down to where the accident was due to "pilot error", but there would be no court-martial, fine, or confinement, and at the same time, I would get what I wanted, relieved of all duties and transferred to an air field to pick up a crew for training, and return to an operational theater.

I hung around, out of sight, for almost two weeks before orders came thru transferring me to Lincoln, Nebraska, where I have to report this coming Thursday. The orders provided for a two-week delay on route.

With the condition I was in, I just had to come home, rest, and get straightened out, or else, the next time I would kill everyone in the plane.

The visit home has been marvelous and I feel better now than when I was in Latrobe. On the way down I stopped at Dyersburg to see Eilers, but was unable to get hold of him. Gurke came over from Gulfport for a one-night visit and I have made arrangements to meet Kent in Shreveport tomorrow night. Now, if they will send me to Rapid City for training, everything will be perfect.

I had been very cool in Columbus and all of us had worn our winter uniforms a couple of weeks, then, on the trip down, it got warm, till halfway down Mississippi, it got hot. This has been a hot week in New Orleans, but the weather feels good to me, even though I notice the heat more than anyone else.

It sure has been lonely around here most of the time as there is no one left I know. Five years now have passed, since I left, and I'm a complete stranger.

                      Love,
                      Bill

I thought that it wouldn't be a bad deal if I could be sent back to England. They had fighter escorts all the way in and out over enemy territory and the invasion forces made it a short walk out if you did go down. I accepted the opportunity to pick up a crew and do a second tour.

I drove to New Orleans and then up to Lincoln, Nebraska, where the crews were formed. I stayed at transient officers' quarters at air bases along the way. On the trip from New Orleans to Lincoln, I stopped at one base and saw my first B-29. I was tempted to go to the base commander and see if I could get my orders changed and fly one of these planes.

On second thought, I didn't do it because I liked to fight like a gentleman. When the day's mission was over, we came back to nice quarters and civilization. The B-29 pilots would come back to a tent on an island in the Pacific. I got in my car and continued on to Lincoln.

Chapter Eleven

New Crew

I went to meet the new crew, this time I had a nine man crew. One of the waist gunners had been eliminated. The one that remained fired both the left and right guns. We went to Sioux Falls, South Dakota for crew training. It was winter of 1944-1945 and cold, but the ground crews kept the planes flying.

One night we went on a navigation mission over North Dakota. My navigator, Bailey, got us lost. I knew it, so I went to his position to check his work. I found him sitting in the bombardier's position looking out. I asked him what he was looking for. "Lights", he replied, "but there is nothing down there, not even Indians."

From the Army Air Base in Sioux City, Iowa:

November 3, 1944

Howdy Marg,

Your letter came thru in quick time even though it went via New Orleans. The answer was held up due to my having so many odd things to do in the off-time to get myself and crew settled.

Lincoln was another wonderful rest. I spent two weeks there playing bridge – enough to last me a year. We used to start at ten in the morning and play till they kicked us out of the club at midnight. All we had to do was meet a twenty-minute formation in the mornings.

They finally gave me a new crew and shipped us up here. I tried my best to be sent to Rapid City, but couldn't swing the deal.

The crew is still too new to tell about them, but I think they will shape up okay. All of the fellows are young and two of them are married. One of them is the radio operator, Wolf, he doesn't have a sister. It seems funny not to have Frank back there.

I just had a letter from Lewis. He and Frank are still "operating" together, which means they are still getting in trouble. We are still close and we hope to get a visit in one way or another.

This is by far the best air field I have ever been on. There is plenty going on all the time. I have been here two weeks and only went to town twice.

Besides the activities, dances, bar, parties, buffet suppers, shows, etcetera, there is good food all the time. I'm getting fatter all the time. Now I weigh about ten pounds more than when you met me.

A lot of fellows ask me why I don't just pick up a crew of returnees and go back across. I'd rather fly here in the U.S. this winter and do my fighting in the spring and summer. The cold air over Germany could kill a man as fast as the flak and fighters, and those night take-offs, with full bomb and gas loads, used to make us sweat plenty. It wouldn't take much ice on a plane like that to make it crash, and it can't be seen in the dark.

Thanks a lot for the clipping. Send me any and all that you see which you think will interest me. How about some of your articles?

Having a crew, and the responsibility that goes with it, is a wonderful feeling again, and there is a lot of work to do. Thank goodness. It's a wonderful feeling to be busy again.

I had a letter from Michelson the other day. I sent him some candy, which he got and used to celebrate his fiftieth mission. He is still flying. I am wondering how much longer Michelson will last.

"Sky Scrapper" went down on her sixty-fourth mission, quite a record for our old plane.

I'm going to sign off now. Some more letters to write and then up at four in the morning for flying. We will be down at noon and off the rest of the day, got to hit that "sack" early.

Love,

Bill

November 15, 1944

Howdy Marg:

Today was a very strenuous one for me. Had to get up at eight-thirty this morning and take an hour of pilot training, then came a big breakfast, the morning paper, and now nothing more to do till tomorrow. It sure is tough getting up at eight-thirty.

There was an article in the paper about a blizzard. Frank and Lewis might have been one of the four hundred that got stuck in town if the blizzard struck at night; otherwise, they were probably in the sack. If they weren't, I bet they are today.

That weather is coming this way. It is now overcast with a strong, cold wind blowing. This is no place for a tropical tramp like me. No snow here yet, but I'm worrying.

The new crew seems to be shaping up pretty good. I've got a good radio operator, again. He gives me plenty of laughs with his sad tales, which are the same I heard when Frank started.

The bombardier is a cocky little flight officer, but he does very good work as armament officer. He really keeps the gunners busy and I believe they are already the best crew in the section.

Our navigator is just out of school and is very neat, quiet and doesn't get bothered when things go wrong.

The copilot had a few hours in a B-17 before coming here, which makes it easy for me. All in all, this crew will probably be better trained when we go overseas than the last one, but only a couple of tough missions can really prove if they are any good at all.

I had a letter from Lewis last week. He is planning on getting married around the first of December. Kent is also planning a wedding in December.

As for me, I have moved around so much since 1939 that I haven't even known a girl long enough to say more than "hello" and "goodbye". A wife would probably give me more responsibility and I would then settle down. It's what I need and is what is best for me, but moving around as much as I have, it seems impossible to even stay in one place and get settled. Besides, staying the short times I do in different places, I usually don't meet any girls I would consider, except for my girl in Ohio.

That doesn't go for you, Marg; you will make a wonderful wife for any man. I wish I had more time in Latrobe. You would be "courted" in great style. Right now though, I will take a snow-check on that bridge game.

We will be at this base till the latter part of January. It continues to be the best I have ever been on. Last week we had a dance on Wednesday night, stag party on Thursday, dance on Saturday, and a buffet supper and dance on Sunday afternoon. That's why we hardly ever go to town.

It is funny to look at the bar here. The place is large, but the only men you see at the brass rail are returnees. A lot of them I didn't know, but we all have mutual friends, and it is a lot of fun swapping lies as we soak up "medicine".

Your last two letters have been exceptionally wonderful, Marg. I could read on, and on, but you always stop for some unknown reason. Ramble all you like, I love it.

Tell your folks and all the gang "hello" for me and take care.

                            Love,

                            Bill

                       December 4, 1944

Howdy Marg:

    Pardon the long delay in this answer to your letter. Besides being just a little busy, there are plenty of social activities, combined with Christmas shopping going on, and it seems like hundreds of letters to answer. Besides writing home, there are my brothers, shipmates from my Navy days, and the whole ex-crew. If I wrote as much as you do every day, I might be able to keep up.

    The newspaper was a pleasant surprise and very enjoyable. Several other fellows read it. They were in Latrobe under the College Training Detachment.

    Everything here is fine, except the weather. We did not have a blizzard, but did have a heavy snow followed by a week of freezing weather. I definitely do not like walking on ice and snow. They should give this land back to the Indians.

We have only been able to fly once or twice a week. Last night was really terrible.

The weather closed in fast, and I tried to get in that way, fast. We had an old plane and could only see out the side, with the window full open. It took me four passes at the field to get in, but even then, I was luckier than one crew who went in on the base leg and took a couple of houses with them. This is rougher than combat.

After landing last night, cleaning up and eating, we all came over to the Officer's Club and had a few good drinks, which were sorely needed.

I have just finished writing Frank. Today noon, I was informed to stand by to go to Rapid City or Ardmore, Oklahoma for flying, because they will have decent flying weather, and this place will be socked-in for awhile. I told them to put me at the head of the list for Rapid City.

Eilers was shipped out of Dyersburg, over a month ago, to Sheppard Field, Texas. As far as I know, quite a few returnees have been shipped there. They are permanently grounded, go thru M.P. school, and then replace the M.P.s who haven't seen active duty. We have several here. They keep their ratings, but lose the wings. It seems funny to see the guard at the gate with the D.F.C., and other decorations, doing a good job. I'm waiting for the drunken night when Eilers has to pull me in.

The only other news about the ex-crew is a rumor concerning Michelson. He was seriously wounded on a raid and the plane crash-landed on the English coast, with only two engines working. No more details.

Now that payday has come and gone, I am wondering if Lewis got married because that was all he was waiting on, according to his last letter. It sure would be swell to get over there and see him settled down. It will give me another home to roll around in.

It won't be long before we are overseas again and I am beginning to get as excited and eager as before. There is nothing going to hold me back now. Not even if Santa brings me what I asked for, "a rich man's play thing". It seems impossible to get a girl that would make a good wife, so I asked Santa for one and am going to hang two beautiful silk stockings Christmas Eve and see if my letter will be answered.

Your card came this morning, Marg. It was really nice. The picture looked good and now it is on the wall, "my pin-up bay". How about the verse? Is that original?

Honest though, I hadn't forgotten you. I have thought of you often, but just didn't get around to writing.

Today is the first Sunday I have had completely free of all formations, flying trainers, and ground school. The afternoon is being spent writing, but at five this will cease and we will proceed with a tea dance, buffet supper, and Cokes with something in them. No alcoholic beverages till after retreat. Everything is closed in town on Sundays, except one private bar for officers. Therefore, we usually have a big time out here at the club.

I hope to do better in the future with my letters to you, Marg. The trouble is, if I write more often the letters will be shorter. Of course, everyone likes to have letters in every mail delivery. Can't blame them because, I'm that way too.

Tell the gang "hello" for me.

For the rest of the family, my best regards.

<blockquote>
For you, the letter and love,
Bill
</blockquote>

<blockquote>December 18, 1944</blockquote>

Howdy Marg:

My trip to Rapid City did not come off as scheduled. Instead, they sent us to Harvard, Nebraska for one night. It was no picnic, because we didn't get to bed till eleven at night, and then, got up at six the next morning to fly another six hours.

The weather has now cleared and reminds me of the winters in New Orleans. There is no snow or ice on the ground, no clouds in the beautiful blue sky, and a nice warm sun shining. It is perfect here on the ground, but very cold when flying.

We had to go to bed early Saturday night, in order to be in shape when the commanding officer woke us at 4:15 for flying yesterday morning. It ruined our Saturday night, but we made up for it last night, by having today off. There was the usual party and buffet supper at the club, but someone went absolutely crazy. They served us free bourbon at the bar for a couple of hours. Even though today is beautiful, none of us feel much like running around.

You shouldn't be anxious to hear from me after every accident you hear about. After I have been overseas a few months, you will be a nervous wreck.

Thanks a lot for the clipping. I had no idea those accidents made such big news. I have been flying at the same time that all the crack-ups occurred and have a pretty good idea what happened to cause the accidents. Most of the trouble is inexperience of the pilots. Even with a thousand hours to my credit; I have still learned a whole lot here and am thankful for the experience.

Thanks a lot for the news about Lewis's wedding. I didn't know whether or not it had come off till your letter.

Neither of them has written me about it, but all three have sent Christmas cards. I sure did want to get over there but couldn't swing the trip. It would have been good to see them serious for a change.

We will be lucky to have even one day off for the holidays if the weather is good enough for flying. Hope your brother's extension comes thru.

Michelson finally came thru with two letters. He wrote about his fateful mission and his wounds. The plane iced up and they went into a spin. The pilot recovered alright. Three crew members bailed out. Then they lost two engines. They made it back to the English coast, but crash-landed because the gear was shot up so bad it wouldn't come down. Michelson got flak in the muscle of his left arm. It took quite a time to heal because there was a lapse of twelve hours between the time he got hit and medical treatment. He is now back at the group, but still grounded. This gives him the Purple Heart, in addition to the Air Medal with six oak leaf clusters, and the Distinguished Flying Cross with two clusters. Quite the "bloody hero", isn't he?

Eilers is now at Lowry Field, Colorado. I don't know what his job is, but he has quit flying. Capt. Wolf, a pilot who was in our squadron overseas, asked him to go up for a ride one day. Eilers refused. Wolf cracked up and was killed on that flight. It made Eilers a confirmed ground lover.

The rest of the guys are all at their same jobs in the same places. Kent was supposed to have been married a few days ago. They sent me an announcement but I haven't heard any more from them.

Even though the present crew is much younger than the last, two of them are married, one is engaged, and the copilot bought a beautiful diamond to give his girl for Christmas.

Marg, I want to wish you the best for this Christmas and a really Happy New Year. Give my best regards to all.

Love,
Bill

Chapter Twelve

1945

January 5, 1945

Howdy Marg:

Here goes the first letter of this year. It would have been written earlier this month, but it took quite some time to recuperate from the holiday.

The partying started Saturday afternoon when a group of officers went to town to do odds and ends. When that was done, we did the rounds of bars and night clubs. They stayed open till two a.m. and really had a festive air, because everything was to be closed up Sunday night.

The big New Year's party was held at the Officers' Club. It was by far the best party I have been to. Nothing was missing, a good band, floor show, plenty of liquor, and everyone I knew. The place was packed, which made it even better.

This past Monday, the gunners wanted all the officers in town for a party. We met okay and had a big time again. It was the first time the whole crew had been out together. They tried to get me drunk and came pretty close to succeeding. I'm going to have to watch them closer in the future.

The weather here has been perfect since Christmas, but much too cold. All of the snow is gone and there is just a little ice. The temperature has been below freezing, all the time, and has dropped below zero a couple of nights. If they continue to keep the ice and snow away, I might get thru the winter up here.

We are practically all thru the work up here. The crew is still going to school, but there is very little flying, and usually I just put in time doing whatever I feel like.

I have gotten back the feeling I had before going over last time, that is, enjoyment in combat flying. I never did get excited about instructing pilots in Columbus.

It's nice flying up there, looking at the beautiful land, and being in the clouds. We haven't had any black clouds for quite a while. As long as they stay away, everything is fine. The ground used to look like a jigsaw puzzle, but now everything fits into a perfect pattern.

I had a letter from Michelson. He is still grounded, but plans to return to flying. I'll kick him in the pants when I get there. Maybe he'll do the same to me. We are nuts!

I also had a letter from Eilers. He went to Sheppard Field, Texas and tried to get overseas duty, but flunked his physical. He is now a truck driver at Lowry Field, Colorado, which is just outside Denver. He says it is quite the town.

Capt. Wolf, who was killed, had just gotten married when he came home from England, about two weeks behind us.

Even after that, I still think combat is safe. Besides him, I had a Christmas letter from another old friend who married an Air Traffic Control pilot; he cracked up and was killed last September, after only a year of married life. Frank, Gay, Kent, in fact all the gunners from the last crew, have written me and their letters are waiting for answers. Still haven't heard from Lewis, but I guess he is still "honeymooning".

I can just see Frank commiserating on his friend's demotion. Frank knows what it is like, and it seems to have done him some good, because he hasn't gotten in trouble again, to my knowledge.

Marg, I sure would like to spend a few days with you again, before going across. Not running around, but just hanging around the house would be a real treat. If everything goes as planned, the dream might become a reality in the latter part of the year. My only New Year's resolution was to get by Latrobe for another visit.

    Tell all the folks and friends "hello" for me and take care.

                                    Love,

                                    Bill

                                East Coast

                                January 26, 1945

Howdy Marg:

    Sorry I haven't written before but they have kept me on the move for quite some time.

    Your letter really surprised me when you said you were looking for me to drop by the end of the month. I meant the end of the year, when I finish this tour and get back home again.

    I'll be back up in your territory because I went and got myself engaged to a girl who lives at Buckeye Lake, Ohio. She is the one I went with all the time I was in Columbus and we have been together three times since. It sure is lonesome without her. We didn't get married because I didn't want to go overseas a married man, and there wasn't anything that was going to keep me in the States. It's hard to be separated again, but I need the excitement of a few combat missions again. After we get married, maybe I'll be able to settle down.

While in Lincoln, I got together with Eilers one afternoon and we really had a wonderful time. He looks good and I am about as fat as he is now. I couldn't kid him about his weight anymore, but he sure did get in some digs. We talked all the time, except while eating two steak dinners and drinking a fifth and a half of whiskey. He had his car but we did very little driving. It sure was good to see him again. I just wished all the old gang was with us. We are planning on a reunion after the war, because there will never be another crew like that one.

You will probably be one sad girl after this letter, Marg. I'm sorry, but I hope you will continue to write, and I really do plan on getting by for a visit. It was a surprise to hear your Mom was even wondering what to cook. When the time comes, tell her not to plan anything. I'll be back in the kitchen eating out the ice box and everything home-cooked tastes wonderful after three years in the army. I don't think any of the boys will be choosy when they get home.

Now that the mail is censored again, it makes it hard to write, because everything that is worthwhile to write about can't be mentioned. They told me there would be days like this.

Well, Marg, I guess I'll close for now with my regards to your folks and the best of everything for you.

Always,

Bill

Upon completion of training, we were sent by train to Camp Kilmer, New Jersey for overseas processing and transportation. We had liberty one night. I went into New York City. I was at a night club, in one of the hotels, and visited the men's room. When I came out, an officer going in said, "Howdy, Cuz!"

I turned and there was my cousin, Tommy. I hadn't seen him since he was going to Louisiana State University, while I was going to Tulane, 1936-1939. I used to visit him at LSU and he stayed with us when he visited New Orleans.

Tommy was a captain in the paratroopers and a company commander. He was also at Camp Kilmer being processed for shipment overseas. We were shipped out together to Scotland on one of the "Queens".

Chapter Thirteen

Europe

When we reached England, I called the 92nd Bomb Group and talked to Colonel McLaughlin, who was now group operations officer. He was a pilot during my first tour and piloted the lead plane on the Schweinfurt mission. He arranged for me and my crew to be assigned to the 407th Squadron of the 92nd Bomb Group.

March 5, 1945

Howdy Marg:

Your first letter, written to the A.P.O. number, reached me at sea, much to my surprise. It must have been brought aboard the night before sailing. The second letter came a few days ago. I would have answered sooner but they have really kept me busy. I'll try to start at the beginning now.

As soon as we arrived in England, I called up the base here and got hold of some of the old-timers. They swung a deal and got me back. I was assigned here because this is where they needed an experienced pilot.

All of the flying personnel have changed, but the ground force is practically the same. The living quarters are not as good, but the food is marvelous. I have even had poorer chow at some bases in the States.

We have only been flying two and a half weeks. I am now a third thru the second tour. It is unbelievable. Frank would enjoy these missions. If I had known things were going to be as easy I would have brought back all old men.

Of course, we do run into trouble. Once I made a two-engine landing and another one laid my navigator up in the hospital. He is in for the D.F.C., besides the

Purple Heart, which he will, positively, be awarded. Even with that, I continue getting fat.

We got over here earlier than I planned and the weather has been bad. It is just starting to improve and it is a relief to have winter behind us.

Another nice thing is our equipment. It is a hundred percent better than before. A lot of things over here are still hard for me to believe.

I stayed in Lincoln for a week, and the night before I left, Eilers found me. He was home on another two week furlough. We had a good time. He had a date and the three of us went out in his car. We drank a fifth and a half of whiskey and ate steak dinners. She couldn't get a word in, edgewise, with us talking all the time.

I'm sorry you went to all that trouble thinking I would be over. Did you drink that bottle of bourbon when you heard I was an engaged man? If not, we will still enjoy it when I return. She might be with me and she might not. She drinks, too, and would enjoy it.

I'll never be able to thank you enough for lighting a candle and praying for me. I'm sure it has helped and will continue to do so. I have never gone in much for religion, but never a day goes by that I don't say my prayers.

Thanks a lot for bringing me up-to-date on all the swell lads and lassies I met in Latrobe. It was good to hear about them and know everyone, and everything, is in pretty good shape. Right now all of us are keeping posted on the floods back in the States.

Michelson left here three weeks before I got back. He was very thin and nervous. The mission, on which he was wounded, did him in. He is recognized as being the "hottest" bombardier to ever be in the Eighth Air Force. He had received six or eight D.F.C.s, innumerable air medals, and a stack of letters of commendation. No one has heard from him since he left England. If you hear anything about him, please pass the info right along.

Well, I've answered both letters, Marg, and am now starting to run out of news. There is probably plenty you want to know. Please ask all the questions possible. I'll answer them if they don't hurt the censorship or security regulations.

Tell all the folks "hello" for me and I hope my next visit won't be as late in the year as originally thought.

As ever,
Bill

Flying the second tour was similar in some ways and different in others. They still got us up early in the mornings. The group briefing, issue of equipment, the truck ride to the plane, the preflight, and then the crew meeting, before enplaning for the mission, were all the same. The number of planes on the mission was greater, as well as, the number of escorting fighters. The sky seemed filled with our aircraft. Before, when the fighter escort over the channel left us, we felt alone and vulnerable. Now the biggest threat to our safety is anti-aircraft fire from the ground. On the first tour we felt safer in the flak because the German fighters left us alone.

On one of the first missions with the new crew, Bailey, our navigator, got lost. I tried to tack on to other groups, up to the time they left the English coast, but never felt comfortable, so I aborted the mission. When we returned to our base, Colonel Wilson, commanding officer, got on the radio and when I told him why I had aborted, he ordered me to fly the assembly once more, so my navigator would never get lost again. That is when the other pilots gave me the nickname "Compass".

I mentioned earlier, about the heavier flak this time compared to the 1943-1944 tour. The Germans seemed to have more guns and they were more accurate. We wore helmets and flak suits, but still, a piece of flak hit Bailey, our navigator, in the calf of his leg. It was a bad wound, and at the time we were on the bomb run. Our bombardier, Cooper, could not help him. I sent down our flight engineer, Baker, and one other to give him first aid. As soon as the bombs were dropped, and the door closed, Cooper helped. We stayed in formation all the way back to our base. Shortly after this, Staley, our copilot, was checked out as first pilot and took over the crew. I was designated a command pilot.

McAfee was another pilot in our squadron who was on his second tour. He was also designated as a command pilot. We were both promoted to the rank of captain.

If our squadron would lead the group, one of us usually flew the lead plane with the squadron commander in the copilot seat. We would sometimes be in the copilot seat, if the squadron did not lead the group. We would also fly in the copilot seat, as deputy commander, to take over the lead if the commander had to abort. This happened once to me. On the bomb run, the squadron commander was having trouble and ordered me to take the lead. I slid over into the lead position and checked with the bombardier to see if he was on target. He assured me he was, so I continued the bomb run to blast a German airfield.

When we returned to our base, the strike photos were checked. The bombardier had missed the target completely.

On one of the Berlin missions, I took over command. We were one of the last groups over the target. It was obscured by smoke. I did a three hundred and sixty degree turn, returned to the IP for another bomb run, dropped two thousand feet, and made a second bomb run. The bombardier still couldn't pick up the target. We went around again, dropped another two thousand feet, and made a third bomb run. This time we dropped our bombs.

After the debriefing, all the crews met in an assembly room. They were all complaining about my leading them three times over Berlin at decreasing altitudes. I countered that we did not lose a plane or a crew member. When Colonel Wilson came in, after examining the strike photos, he said we had hit our target under adverse conditions, without loss of life or plane, so it was a successful mission. We had hit our target!

April 11, 1945

Howdy Marg:

This is the most beautiful day England has ever had. There isn't a cloud in the sky and the good old sun is really beating down. We ran around outdoors in our shirt sleeves, and with less than that on when inside. If I hadn't just come back from pass, I would have enough energy to enjoy it.

My last letter found me a third of the way thru this tour. Well, this letter finds me two-thirds of the way thru, plus four missions to London.

If they continued flying me like they did when I first came over, I could be on my way back home again.

Instead, my copilot has been checked out and has taken over the crew.

I only fly when our squadron leads, and then I'm in the copilot seat as group, or deputy group, air commander. You can ask Frank what that is, Marg.

My tour consists of thirty missions. I have volunteered for fifteen extras, but the war will probably end before I can even finish the thirty. It doesn't make any difference because our opposition is practically nil, which suits me fine.

Yes, I saw "Winged Victory." Of course, I thought it terrible, no B-17s. The similarity of names was peculiar.

My navigator, Bailey, is now a very happy fellow. They have put a "shipping cast" on his leg and he expects to go home any day now. They let him run all over the hospital in a wheel chair.

I've just gotten a letter from my cousin, Sis, the nurse. Her brother, Tommy, a captain in the paratroopers, jumped into combat one morning and was in the hospital wounded in two places that evening. They haven't seen each other since 1939.

I saw her on my last tour here and he came over on the same boat I did. It was the first time we had seen each other since 1937. We all went to grammar school together in Panama.

The only time I heard a v-bomb in London was on my second visit. The damn thing nearly knocked me out of bed. Outside of disturbing my sleep, it didn't bother me at all.

I did lose some weight when I first came over. My chest got back up in position. Now, with the easy life, it is starting to slip down again and my weight is going up.

I have also heard from Kent. He is still at the same field but is now a gunnery instructor on B-29s.

Price, our copilot, is now an instructor at Dyersburg and Gay flies with him quite often.

That brings the news of the crew and me up to date.

My regards to all the family.

                        As ever,

                        Bill

The last combat mission I flew was to Rosenheim, Germany, April 18, 1945. I was deputy squadron leader. Jackson was my copilot. We were the lead squadron of the group. It felt strange to me that the target was Rosenheim. Was this the town Grandfather Rose left so many years ago to escape conscription, and from which he took the name "Rose"?

Bombers were of no use the last few weeks of the war, as the ground troops were moving fast and we might bomb our own men. We just sat back and waited for the end, V-E Day, May 8, 1945.

It was over!

Chapter Fourteen

Army of Occupation

When our men were liberated from prisoner of war camps, they were taken to American staging camps set up on the West Coast of France. The camps were named after cigarettes, Lucky Strike, Old Gold, Camel, Chesterfield, etcetera. Here the former prisoners had physical examinations and were identified before being released, to be sure a German did not substitute himself for one of our men.

I was one, from our group, that visited the camps to try to identify our former members. I was able to pick out one. When he and others were identified, they were released in our custody and flown back to the base from which they had left so long ago. They were given priority transportation home, which took a couple of days to arrange.

The army set up a point system. Those with the lowest numbers were sent directly to the Pacific. Many went via the United States and were there at V-J Day, and consequently, were discharged first. The groups with the middle numbers were kept in Europe, as the Army of Occupation. The high point men were flown home to be discharged. The high point Air Corps men, of which I was one, stayed and did the flying.

Our group removed all the armament of the B-17s and put in wood benches, along both sides, and in the bomb bay. The group was moved from Podington, England to Istres, France, on the Mediterranean coast. We lived in tents on a former German air base.

To clear the base of land mines, a local shepherd was hired to bring his flock onto the base and lead them over the entire area. He was compensated for each sheep that was killed.

The last training flight I had, out of England, was a night navigational mission, north to the Norwegian Sea. At this time of year, we saw the sun set and twilight move from West to East, around the Northern horizon, and become dawn.

June 6, 1945

Howdy Marg:

It sure has been a busy time since I got a letter to you. I'm now going to stand in the corner for five minutes and repent.

You know a lot has happened since my last letter. The biggest and main thing was the end of the war over here – at last.

It found me with fifty-four missions to my credit and high man in the group. Michelson topped my record by four, but he is no longer here. We were all glad to see the end and we had a two-day party.

After that, they announced our new job. Since we are one of the oldest groups in England, they are keeping us over here as part of the Army of Occupation, while the newer groups are going home, get a short leave, training, and then over to the Pacific for more combat.

We will be based in Southern France. No, not around the beautiful part everyone thinks about, but in the middle of thirty-five miles of nothing. The place has been described to us as similar to an area about fifteen miles outside of Tucson, Arizona. We will be living in tents, and from all reports, it is really a hell hole.

Our new job will be transport. They have to get combat out of all the pilots' systems and teach us to be safe passenger pilots. That called for an extensive training program. The planes fly twenty-four hours a day. It hasn't been bad on me though, because I've been working in the operations office, fighting the paper war.

The past few days haven't been so nice. They put me in charge of loading cargo and the planes aren't built for it. Besides that, it's still rainy all the time, and it never gets warm over here. We have been wet, cold, and covered with mud all this week.

I have managed to get up in the air a couple of times. Once was right after V-E Day. We flew over Holland and Belgium one night. They still didn't have electricity, but they made up for it with fireworks, flares, rockets, and search lights. It was a beautiful flight.

Just a few nights ago, I was up on top of the clouds and it was beautiful. We took off at eleven at night and there was a twilight, which moved from the West, around to the North, and East, becoming dawn by the time we landed at three in the morning.

Another flight was to Camp Lucky Strike in France. We went over and spent the whole day. A day that none of us will ever forget.

Lucky Strike is a tent camp thrown up to accommodate all the men who were in German prison camps. There is one section for the Air Corps, where we hung out.

The men do nothing but stand around all day, just like you see them in the movies. Each of us always had a crowd around us. They would stand in one place for hours, just listening to every word we spoke. For many of them, we were the first person they had spoken to, or heard talk, since going down, except their fellow prisoners. They were the most patient, soft spoken bunch of men I have ever seen. All of them had questions to ask. Some wanted to know if their formations had come thru, others asked if their outfits were still in England, while others wondered if some old buddy was still around. It was impossible to answer most of their questions.

The best part of the whole thing was to see the fellows we knew from our own outfit. A lot of them we had seen go down during '43 and '44.

Tell Frank, his friend, Brubaker, is now on his way home and have him tell Lewis that, Thompson, a navigator, is also headed back to the states.

A lot of the men got seven-day leaves in England and we flew a plane load back, while others have been paying us visits here, everyday. Out of the bunch I flew back, about twelve of them were from this group and had gone down during January and February '44. They were now landing at the same field where they had taken-off fifteen months earlier. It was wonderful to see their joy and excitement.

I haven't been to any of the places where the crew used to go on pass. What few passes I have had, I spent in London. Each time I saw a good stage show, a cinema, and consumed my share of scotch. The best leave of all was spent in Belfast. Did I tell you about that?

My brother, Charlie, joined the Navy when he was seventeen and he will be nineteen this month. In his two years of service in the Navy, he has been to sea only once for a very short period. All the rest of the time he goes to schools.

First to one on the East coast, then one on the West coast, and then back to another on the East coast. All he does is travel back and forth across the continent. Every once in a while he gets home for a few days. Once they stopped him halfway and stuck him in a school in Chicago. He has just finished a course in San Francisco and is now awaiting assignment. He is a torpedo man second class, which is good.

There was an article in the "Stars and Stripes", which I cut out for you, but have now lost. It was a list of all those who received French Decorations. Michelson was awarded the Croix de Guerre.

Cornwell is the only one of the crew I have heard from. He is still a ground gunnery instructor at Walla Walla, Wash.

What have you heard about the gang?

Well, Marg, this about brings me up to date again. I'll try not to take so long answering your next letter. Please excuse me this time.

Tell all your folks "hello" for me and it looks as if our next get together won't be till the middle or later part of '46.

Always,
Bill

One flight I had been on was to Weisbaden, Germany, where I visited my cousin, Sis. This was our first visit on my second tour. She was now a Mrs., having been married the month after I left England, at the end of my first tour. During my first tour, I visited her several times in London and met her fiancé. I visited her another time on a trip to Norwich, England. She was with the 30th General Hospital. During the first tour, if there was a mission with seriously wounded aboard, the planes would land on the coast to get the wounded to a hospital as soon as possible. If they had a lot of patients after a mission, she would call me at Podington to see if I was a survivor, for her own peace of mind.

Back to Istres and the Green Project as it was known. We would carry thirty-five to forty infantrymen in a plane and fly from France, down the East coast of Spain, through the Straits of Gibraltar, and then down the West coast of Morocco to Casablanca. The infantrymen deplaned there. They were then taken by MATS, Military Air Transport Service, to Brazil, for refueling, and then on to Miami, Florida. Our planes flew on to Port Lyautey, where they remained overnight. The next morning each plane was loaded with French families who wanted to return to their native country.

From Istres, we ran "Liberty Runs" to England, Paris, and Rome.

When I was assigned to fly one of the flights to Rome, I arranged for my cousin to come to Istres the day before. She stayed overnight at a nearby clinic and got to the airport in time to leave with me the next morning. She had the bombardier's seat in the nose for takeoff and landing and flew part of the time in the copilot's seat.

After a couple of months at Istres, I was sent to Port Lyautey as operations officer. My job was to take care of planes and crews overnight, to see that the planes were properly loaded, left on time the next morning, and to train the backup crews who were rotated weekly in Ground Control Approach. I really enjoyed this instructing.

July 6, 1945

Howdy Marg:

Here I am writing you from the third continent this year. I wonder how many more I will get to visit.

They now have me located on the West coast of Africa. It is really wonderful, too. The sun shines all the time, and since we are right on the ocean, there is a fine, cool breeze blowing. That sun is the best thing after living in England.

How did I get here? It all happened very fast. I came back from a two-day pass last Wednesday, at noon, and at one-thirty they had me on a plane headed for Southern France with all my baggage.

The next morning they shipped me out again for this place, via Casablanca. Ever since arriving, I have been the best operations officer for the Eighth Air Force in Africa. I can't help it if I am the only one.

As you know, going into a new job takes quite a bit of time to get settled and we are just reaching that stage. They haven't let me alone long enough to enjoy any daytime sports, but they haven't been able to keep me around at night.

Our club is in town and I haven't been able to drag myself away. They serve nothing but cold, bottled, American beer. After the English mild and bitter, served warm, this is a treat that can't be passed up. There is no scotch. No, they don't have a drop. Instead, we have to drink that old American bourbon and they mix it with ice and real Cokes bottled back in the U.S.A. You can see why they will have to blast me off this post.

The food is one thing everyone in the Army worries about. We worry here, too, because our appetites might not be too good at meal time. We have fresh eggs, fruits and vegetables. That is the kind of stuff we have been dreaming about since leaving the States.

I got notice of my promotion over the air on the last day of May. I was sitting down on the end of the runway, waiting to take off, with Stroud as my copilot. They called me up from the tower, on the radio, and made the great announcement. All the other fellows flying heard it and they all called in with congrats. The air was sure busy there for a little while. Stroud is a captain, and as soon as we were airborne, I threw my old bars out the window and put his on. That was the day I flew over to the camp where the released P/Ws were staying and brought the load back with us. You can imagine what kind of a party we had that night, because it was also payday.

What has happened to that first bunch of bums that used to fly with me? Not a one has written in the past two months and all of them owe me a letter. Get on Frank for me please, Marg.

Our group is now busy transporting troops, and when this job is done, we will be sent to Germany as part of the Occupational Force. What a future we have to look forward to. Most of our fellows have enough points to be discharged, but there are no replacements or transportation for us. Tell Frank I have one hundred and six points that aren't doing me a bit of good and I will gladly lend him all he needs till someone sees fit to send me back.

My pass in Belfast was really wonderful because they have pure food laws and we can eat anything and everything. The most important thing was drinking fresh milk. We nearly drowned ourselves in the stuff. At night, we all had more than one date. The girls and people really treat the Americans swell, and there are several very good night clubs. During the day we just bummed around and tried to buy some linen, but the prices were too high.

It was good to hear you have taken up driving as another of your accomplishments. Which side of the road do you drive on? That sounds like I might be pulling your leg, as the English say, but often I have to figure it out. England is left-handed drive. Now, try to figure out how many times I have changed from driving on one side to the other.

We had a dance at the club last Saturday and one on the fourth of July. They can't get me away from the bar even with a sledge hammer. There aren't many girls who attend because we only allow the French and they don't think much of us. We're trying to get them around to our way of thinking. A good formal dance, back in the States, would be pretty good along about now.

Thanks a lot for the picture of the bums. Tell Frank to dig up some prints for me. I haven't even seen a picture of Lewis's wife, as well as some others they must have taken.

I tried writing this by typewriter to see if these new fangled gadgets can spell better than my pen, but it doesn't look like it. Best the salesman gets this one back.

This isn't using as many pages as the others, but there is quite a bit here. It has taken me from noon till supper time to get it written.

Tell all the folks "hello" for me and write soon.

As always,
Bill

August 20, 1945

Howdy Marg:

Here's that long awaited letter in answer to your two. They have kept me running around too fast to write. Two weeks ago today, I flew down to Casablanca and Lyautey. I came back Tuesday, left Wednesday, returned Friday night, left Sunday morning for England, and didn't get back till last night. It was really a glorious two weeks.

Rome is the best town I have been in so far. Two days weren't enough to see everything. Two weeks would have been better.

The Air Force has a group of hotels, right in the center of town for a rest camp, and it was just like Miami Beach or any other redistribution center. Good food, music with every meal, and a well stocked bar. The room and three meals a day cost fifty cents.

There are a lot of wonderful places to visit in and around the city, but I couldn't even start to see them all. The most interesting thing I did see was the cemetery of the Capuchin Fathers. Have you ever heard of it?

Each hotel had a dance every night, and the girls that are allowed in belong to the big shots of the Allied Commission. They all speak English and were sights for dust-filled eyes.

They sent me up to England for three days, as traffic controller, as we switched a thousand men each way. We used a permanent fighter field as the transfer point and the living quarters were swell, but that weather beats me. It is still cold, wet and just plain "stinky". It took us a whole week to do three days work.

It felt good to get back down here in the sunshine and go swimming. I spent the whole afternoon out at the beach today.

The first round of the Jap surrender came while I was waiting for the plane in Rome. Somebody broke open a bottle and we all had a drink. Then we continued the party here at Istres. The fighter boys in England were no peahens, so we celebrated for a couple of days up there. It feels good to spend a quiet evening in the barracks for a change.

Now that I'm over here, I really want to see the place. So far it has been very good. If I see it all now I will never want to come back.

On our return trips we carry French refugees. Most of them are babies and they make quite a problem. It's funny to see the radio operators and engineers holding babies in their arms during take-offs and landings. Some of them have even learned how to change diapers. Frank would sure love that.

All of our eighty-five point and over ground officers and enlisted men have now been replaced, and the fellows are on their way home after three years of service. The flying enlisted men, who have the required number of points, will leave in a few days, but there is no word when they will replace the high-point flying officers. We feel like strangers in our own outfit, there are so many new faces around.

I am wondering if Frank and Lewis have now been discharged. Gurke has gotten out on a medical discharge.

Michelson writes that he is at Drew Field, Tampa, doing nothing. He also said Price was killed in a head-on collision between Dyersburg and Memphis. Combat is pretty safe after all.

Kent writes that he is still at Shreveport doing the same kind of instructing on B-29s. He's looking forward to being discharged and has his post-war plans already made out.

My gal in Ohio is pretty good. She works at night, which makes me very happy. She writes almost daily and sends quite a few pictures. I got one today and have been staring at it all evening. She looks wonderful to me and I sure do miss her. The love bug must really have me.

Too bad you didn't know it before you went for a visit in Detroit, but I have a namesake there who is married to a beautiful

Canadian girl. They are my age and a lot of fun. We even look alike. I spent twenty-four hours with them once, the latter part of '39.

I read "First of the Many" while stationed in Africa. It is really good. My latest reading was "Green Years" by A.J. Cronin. It was pretty good, but nothing to compare to "The Citadel".

This about brings me up to date on everything from this end. Next time I'll answer your letter sooner.

Tell everyone "hello" for me.

Bill

Since we were on a naval base, I got to know some of the naval personnel. They took me for a blimp ride and let me handle the flight controls. We flew down to Casablanca and went up and down the streets at about twenty to thirty miles an hour. We waved to the people on the roof tops. Some were cooking and we could smell the aroma of their food.

To reciprocate, when I had to "slow-time" an engine for two hours, whenever we installed a new engine, I would take along any navy personnel who wanted to go. Once in the air, I gave them the controls and let them fly the plane. They thought the B-17 was a fighter. They would dive, climb and make sharp turns. Well, it was an interesting way to spend two hours going nowhere.

One day we took a plane to the Rock of Gibraltar for a steak and egg lunch and shopping at the "Hindu" stores. It reminded me of Front Street in Colon, Panama.

Around the first of October, I was transferred to Frankfurt, Germany as operations officer for an Air Force detachment that was set up to fly Greek DPs (displaced persons) home. I met my commanding officer at Istres and we flew up together. He was from Texas. When we landed in Germany, I climbed on his motorcycle and we took off looking for bullets and food for our crews. When I heard that some DPs had threatened our crews, I secured Colt 45 pistols and ammunition and armed our flight crews. We kept the Greeks in the rear of the plane. I instructed our men that if any of the passengers tried to enter the radio room they were to be shot. Evidently, just arming the crews kept peace on the flights.

Come to find out, they were being returned against their wishes, as these Greeks had left voluntarily, or with the German army of their own free will. They were going to be prosecuted as traitors when they returned. Sure enough, in Athens our planes were met by trucks with armed guards who carted off our passengers to who knows where.

One afternoon in October, an unscheduled plane came in from Istres. When I asked the pilot what his plans were, he said, "I am your replacement. You are going home!"

I flew his plane back to Istres. Then a group of us were flown to a fighter base in England where we spent several weeks before boarding the "Queen Mary" for the trip home.

October 24, 1945

Howdy Marg:

Here I sit in England writing you again. That shouldn't be, but someone must think I like this place.

Yep, I'm right in front of a coke fire with one side of me warm and the other freezing. Best maybe I begin at the beginning.

My last job on the continent was as a 40th Bomb Wing Detachment operations officer in Munich, Germany. Twelve planes a day left Istres, France after lunch and got to us by supper time, where they spent the night. The following morning, we loaded them with Greek DPs and sent them to Athens where they spent the second night, and then returned to Istres the third day.

I was there for a week and we really worked. During the day, while no planes were in, we were battling with the Third Army for transportation, quarters, and food.

Then one day, an extra plane came in. On board was a replacement for me. I was going home.

I went back to Istres for a few days and then to England, to this fighter group. We arrived the twenty-eighth of September and we were to sail home on the tenth of October.

On the sixth they cancelled our shipment and said we were going to sail on the eighteenth or on the twenty-first. They soon cancelled those shipments and gave us a new sailing date of November fourth. Now, that has been scrubbed and we will probably sail after the middle of the month.

What do the people back in the states think when we tell them not to write, that we are on our way home, and then we don't get there for two months? We flew over forty thousand infantrymen home, ten thousand French refugees to France, and three thousand Greeks from Germany, but we ourselves cannot fly, or be flown, while the planes sit on the ground and rot. What a way to have "the brass" show their appreciation for what we have done.

In this fighter group, waiting for a boat, are men with ninety points and over, and thirty-five years of age and older.

We have been living off the post, in a big manor house. The only trouble is, all the furniture was moved out in anticipation of our first sailing date, and there is nothing left in the rooms but the beds. We live out of suitcases and have our clothes hung on wire which we stretched across the room. Friday we are moving onto the field in some tumbled- down old shacks.

There is absolutely nothing for us to do day and night. We go to London, once a week, for a couple of days, and see all the shows there. Then we spend the rest of our time seeing the shows in Ipswich and Felixstowe. There isn't a show in England I haven't seen.

Do you want; a murder committed, to escape from prison, to make love in a hundred different ways, to stage a robbery, or anything at all? Just ask me how. I've learned how from the screen.

Has Frank been able to get out of the Army yet? I imagine so. Has he heard from any of the others? They all stopped writing, except Kent, with V-E Day.

Thanks for the invitation to the homecomings. I hope to be up in that part of the country shortly after I get back to the States. That should be around Christmas, but I hate the cold climate. What am I worrying about? I will probably still be here in England till summer, waiting for a boat. Anyway, I'll do my best to get by and see you all again.

Have you met with your fiancé yet? How did everything turn out? I'm really curious.

As for my "love life", it isn't going so well. We have been separated a long time. I'm sort of glad at times, but am wondering how she feels. That's what she gets for liking an irresponsible "cod" like me. Maybe it's a good thing we were separated so long.

Now it has gotten late again and the room is just beginning to get warm. Soon I'll "hit the rack", up for breakfast (powdered eggs), play snooker, eat lunch, read, sleep, clean up, eat supper, go to town to a show, and "back to the rack". It sure does get tiresome. Too bad we can't have all this free time back in the States.

There's not much use in sending the answer to this over here. Our mail is being stopped somewhere and returned to the senders. Best you write me at the New Orleans address. They are sending me to Camp Shelby for separation and I'll go home before heading north. Have to go to Ohio and find out whether or not I'm going to be a married man.

Tell everyone "hello" for me and I'll see you soon – I hope.

As ever,
Bill

Chapter Fifteen

Dance

Armistice Day

Dear Bill:

More than ever – I was wishing I could get a letter to you overseas because, Mister, you really needed mail – but, by now you're probably relaxed, inhaled that New Orleans air and thought "Here, this is more like it!"

It must have been unpleasant to wait around for the ship that doesn't come in – our brother Jim was in the same boat (that's an ironic statement). We've been expecting him for two months and he still isn't home but we're hoping, again, that it will be this week.

Frank is home now and here's his message to you... "Tell him all about me – tell him I wish he was here – that I'd take him out and get him drunk." So there, now you know he's home in full force. It is now 8:30 p.m. and he just got home from a football game that ended at 5 p.m. He was discharged from Andrew Field, Maryland on October 24 and it's grand having him home again – just as nice as it is having Bob- another brother who was discharged from the same base last week.

They've really pepped us all up- their round table discussions after supper are just like old times.

Frank hasn't started back to work as yet but is considering it – of course that will probably take two or three more weeks deliberation.

Frank is up to his old tricks. He's been celebrating with Hank – that sailor friend of his that you met at Helen's - and Bill – the Marine you also met there. Hank's home on leave and Bill has been discharged.

Bill, I was really sorry to hear that things weren't working out as well between you and the little gal at Buckeye Lake. Everything may be alright once you are here again – separations do things to people – just ask me. Maybe you were just despondent about getting home and for that reason thought everything was going wrong.

As for my fiancé and I - well, I've seen him – often – since I last wrote to you. He came home on September eleventh. I knew he was in town and was almost frantic about meeting him out in a crowd- but I needn't have been – because two days later he called Mom (not me) and asked if he could come up. Our house was the first place he came to – because he felt the same way I did about the whole thing. He was on thirty days leave at the time – and I saw him practically every day.

Since that time he has been discharged and has settled himself in a very fine job at the American Locomotive Company office in town.

I'm not wearing the diamond he gave me, – I figured I'd better not rush into things – he has really changed - not nearly as serious as he used to be - and that is the way I'd like to have him stay.

Bill, I sure hope that you'll plan to visit with us for awhile – we're kind of counting on it – and will be disappointed if you don't make it a point to stop here. We're anxious to get a gander at you in civilian clothes, which is secondary to enjoying a visit again.

I think Frank is surprised that you and I have kept up this correspondence as we have but I can truthfully say that it's the easiest thing in the world to write to you, Bill, and I've read and re-read your letters many times.

I know how you must have felt sitting over there in England all that time, but isn't it swell to be home now, and it's just so good for the people back home who were waiting for you to get here.

So, please come – and write soon.

As ever,
"Marg"

I arrived home in New Orleans just in time for Thanksgiving.

Then off to Buckeye Lake, Ohio to pick up my car, which I had left with my girl. My car was in place of an engagement ring. I had a real change of heart.

As soon as I got my car, we said our sad goodbyes, and I left.

I called Marg, in Latrobe, and asked her for a date.
She said, "Sure, come on over."

I arrived Saturday night, December 1, 1945. We went to Eastwood Inn, in Ligonier, one of Marg's favorite places, with Marg's brother, Frank, my radioman on the first crew, her brother, Bob, and their dates.

After sitting at the bar awhile, Marg said, "Bill, I have never danced with you."

So, I asked her to dance.

We went out on the small dance floor, in another room, and picked out a tune on the juke box.

We danced.

We looked at each other, while still dancing to the soft music, and I asked Marg, "You know why I am here, don't you?"

Though she was totally taken by surprise, she gave me the answer I was hoping for, "Yes".

I paused, collected my thoughts, and said, "Will you marry me?"

"Yes!"

We kissed for the first time!

I told Marg I was hoping we could be married and go home to New Orleans for Christmas, since I had not been with my family, over the holidays, for four years. Marg said she did not know how she could ever get it done so quickly, but she was excited to make all the arrangements for our marriage.

We decided it was best to tell Marg's parents the great news the following morning. I am sure her brothers sensed a new dimension to our relationship that evening, especially her brother, Frank, my radioman.

☆☆☆☆☆

Marg's mother remembered my visit back in 1944 and how much I loved her cooking. She planned a special dinner for my visit this time, too. Marg's mother was so excited about our news that she forgot to put salt in the rolls she was baking. I was surprised she did not forget the whole meal.

Marg's father pleaded with us to wait six months, until we were sure and I had settled myself into a job. I convinced her father that I wanted to start a new life and I wanted to start it with his daughter. He told me they did not object to me, it was just so sudden. Once her parents realized we were standing firm, they gave us their blessing.

☆☆☆☆☆

We called to surprise my parents with the great news. They agreed that since it was going to be a small wedding service, they would not come to Latrobe, but we would celebrate at home in New Orleans at Christmastime. They were thrilled and anxious to meet my new wife.

A few days later, I left to see my uncle in New York City about a job with the airlines. The job did not work out, but while I was there, I decided to try to find a suit. Civilian clothes' production had sharply decreased during the war years, a nice suit was hard to find. Lucky for me, I found two and some other civilian clothes.

I called a friend of my parents, who also lived in New York City, and she helped me pick out a beautiful engagement ring and wedding ring for Marg.

Five days later, I returned to Latrobe to help Marg finalize our wedding plans. Marg had the plans well underway. She had given notice at work, gotten dispensation from the priest - she said you had to do that during Advent - chose her attendant, and had gone to Pittsburgh, to buy her wedding outfit.

News got around fast, in Latrobe, that Marg was getting married to an out-of-town pilot and taking off for New Orleans. Parties filled the next few evenings; I think they wanted to check out Marg's "flyboy".

Something funny happened when we went to get our marriage license. They asked where we were born.

Marg replied, "Latrobe".

They turned to me, "Where were you born?"

I told them the truth, "Tela, Honduras."

Marg looked at me in shock and asked, "Where?"

We had gotten to know each other over a period of two years through correspondence, but apparently, we still had a lot to learn about each other. I promised her that all of her questions would be answered as we made our way down south to New Orleans, after our wedding.

After our whirlwind courtship of two weeks, we were married on December 15, 1945, in the rectory of Marg's church. Frank, my radioman and Marg's brother, served as my best man.

We left Mountain View Inn, in Greensburg, following our wedding breakfast that Marg's parents were kind enough to host for us. We started our trip to New Orleans. We were going home. Our worldly, possessions fit into two suitcases.

Once at home in New Orleans, I will take off my tie, roll up my shirt sleeves, put my feet under a table, and relax. Whenever I get tired of that, I will just roll around on the floor and absorb a little of that good old home atmosphere.

For my wife and for this marvelous country,

Bill

Acknowledgements

This book has been a loving journey. It would not have been possible if I had not been left a small stack of letters tucked away in a shoebox, with my name on it. I thought how nice it would be to compile those letters with my parent's memoirs, *"Decisions, Decisions, Decisions"* memoir of William B. Rose and *"Distant Recall"* memoir of Mary Margaret Cline Rose. The memoirs were written by Marg and Bill and the information contained in them is assumed to be their writings and not the writings of any outside source, except where noted.

While on this journey, why not gather more information on WWII, most especially, the Eighth Air Force, 92nd Bombardment Group. *92nd USAAF-USAF Memorial Association*: Operations Journals. An article: *Fighters Escort Lame Fort Back*, The Times-Picayune, April 11, 1944, p.11, is reproduced in this book.

My fascination grew and the book became a historical account. That is not what my mother had always wanted. She wanted their *story* to be written. With editing, their story rose from the pages and the remainder was edited away for future writings.

I would like to thank all of the contributors to the many websites and books I used as references. I am happy to note them here. *The Authentic History Center* website: www.authentichistory.com. *Wrong Place! Wrong Time!* by George C. Kuhl, Schiffer Military/Aviation History, 1993. Used as mentioned in William B. Rose's memoir. The History Channel website: www.history.com. *The Savage Sky*, Life and Death on a Bomber over Germany in 1944, George Webster, Stackpole Books, 2007. *Masters of the Air*, America's Bomber Boys Who Fought The Air War Against Nazi Germany, Donald L. Miller, Simon and Schuster Paperbacks, 2006. *The Mighty Eighth in WWII*, A Memoir, Brig. Gen. J. Kemp McLaughlin, USAFR (Ret.), The University Press of Kentucky, 2000. Thank you for documenting our nation's history.

It is with heartfelt gratitude that I thank all servicemen and servicewomen for protecting us and this marvelous country.

Thank you to all of the servicemen and women mentioned in this book, especially my uncle, Frank Cline.

For more information on military history and to join the
92nd USAAF-USAF Memorial Association:
Please follow this link to their website:
www.92ndma.org

Made in the USA
Charleston, SC
18 December 2009